A

JANE AUSTEN

CHRISTMAS

REGENCY CHRISTMAS
TRADITIONS

Maria Grace

White Soup Press

Published by: White Soup Press

For information, address
author.MariaGrace@gmail.com

ISBN-10: 0692332332
ISBN-13: 978-0692332337 (White Soup Press)

Author's Website: RandomBitsofFaascination.com
Email address: **Author.MariaGrace@gmail.com**

Dedication

For my husband and sons.
You have always believed in me.

Table of Contents

i

Celebrating a Jane Austen Christmas

Each year the holiday season seems to begin earlier and earlier. Complaints about holiday excesses and longings for 'simpler' and 'old fashioned' holiday celebrations abound. But what exactly does an 'old fashioned Christmas' really look like?

Many Christmas traditions and images of 'old fashioned' holidays are based on Victorian celebrations. Going back just a little further, to the beginning of the 19th century, the holiday Jane Austen knew would have looked distinctly odd to modern sensibilities.

How odd? Families rarely decorated Christmas trees. Festivities centered on socializing instead of gift-giving. Festivities focused on adults, with children largely consigned to the nursery. Holiday events, including balls, parties, dinners, and even weddings celebrations, started a week before Advent (the fourth Sunday before Christmas) and extended all the way through to Twelfth Night in January.

1

As today, not everyone celebrated the same way or observed all the same customs, but many observances were widely recognized. Some of the traditions and dates that might have been observed included:

Stir it up Sunday
On the fifth Sunday before Christmas, the family would gather to 'stir up' Christmas puddings that needed to age before serving at Christmas dinner.

December 6th: St. Nicholas Day
In a tradition from Northern Europe, the day might be celebrated with the exchange of small gifts, particularly for children. House parties and other Christmastide visiting also began on or near this day.

December 21st: St. Thomas Day
Elderly women and widows went 'thomasing' at the houses of their more fortunate neighbors, hoping for gifts of food or money. Oftentimes landowners cooked and distributed wheat, an especially expensive commodity, to the 'mumpers' who came begging.

December 24th: Christmas Eve
Holiday decorating happened on Christmas Eve when families cut or bought evergreen boughs to deck the house. The greenery remained in place until Epiphany when it was removed and burned lest it bring bad luck.

December 25th: Christmas day
Families typically began the day with a trip to church and might pick up their Christmas goose from the local baker on the way home. Though gifts were

not usually exchanged on Christmas, children might receive small gifts and cottagers might give generous landowners a symbolic gift in appreciation of their kindness.

The day culminated in a much anticipated feast. Traditional foods included boar's head, brawn, roast goose, mince meat pies, and the Christmas puddings made a month earlier.

THE CHRISTMAS DINNER.
~Peter Parley, *Tales about Christmas*

December 26th: Boxing Day

After receiving their Christmas boxes, servants usually enjoyed a rare day off. Churches distributed the money from their alms-boxes.

Families might attend the opening day of panto-mimes. The wealthy traditionally enjoyed fox hunting on this day.

December 31: New Year's Eve

Families thoroughly cleaned the house before gathering in a circle before midnight to usher out the old year and in the new.

Some Scots and folks of northern England believed in 'first footing'—the first visitor to set foot across the threshold after midnight on New Year's Eve affected the family's fortunes. The 'first footer' entered through the front door and left through the back door, taking all the old year's troubles and sorrows with him.

Jan 1: New Year's Day

The events of New Year's Day predicted the fortunes for the coming year, with a variety of traditions said to discern the future like 'creaming the well', or the burning of a hawthorn bush.

Jan 6th: Twelfth Night

A feast day honoring the coming of the Magi, Epiphany or Twelfth Night, marked the traditional climax of the holiday season and the time when celebrants exchanged gifts.

Revels, masks and balls were the order of the day. With the rowdy games and large quantities of highly alcoholic punch, they became so raucous that Queen Victoria outlawed Twelfth Night parties by the 1870's.

The Joys of Plum Pudding

"Hallo! A great deal of steam! The pudding was out of the copper [boiler]. A smell like washing–day! That was the cloth [the pudding bag]. A smell like an eating house and a pastrycook's next door to each other, with a laundress's next door to that! That was the pudding!

In half a minute Mrs. Cratchit entered—flushed, but smiling proudly—with the pudding. Like a speckled cannon ball, so hard and firm, blazing in half of half-a-quartern of ignited brandy, and bedight with Christmas holly stuck into the top."

"Oh, a wonderful pudding! Bob Cratchit said, and calmly too, that he regarded it as the greatest success achieved by Mrs. Cratchit since their marriage..."

Charles Dickens~A Christmas Carol

Origins of Plum Pudding

Plum pudding stands out as one of the few foods that can trace its history back at least eight hundred years. It began in Roman times as a pottage, a meat and vegetable concoction prepared in a large cauldron, to which dried fruits, sugar and spices might be added.

Porridge or *frumenty* appeared in the 14th century. Eaten during the days preceding Christmas celebrations, the soup-like fasting dish contained meats, raisins, currants, prunes, wine and spices. By the 15th century, *plum pottage,* a soupy mix of meat, vegetables and fruit often appeared at the start of a meal.

As the 17th century opened, frumenty evolved into a plum pudding. Thickened with eggs and breadcrumbs, the addition of beer and spirits gave it more flavor and increased its shelf life. Suet gradually replaced meat in the recipe and the root vegetables disappeared.

By 1650, plum pudding had transformed from a main dish to the customary Christmas dessert. Not long afterward though, Oliver Cromwell banned plum pudding because he believed the ritual of flaming the pudding resembled pagan celebrations of the winter solstice.

George I, sometimes called the Pudding King, revived the dish in 1714 when he requested plum pudding as part of the royal feast celebrating his first Christmas in England. As a result, it regained its place in traditional holiday celebrations.

In the 1830's it took its final cannon-ball form, made with flour, fruits, suet, sugar and spices, all topped with holly and flaming brandy. Anthony Trollope's *Doctore Thorne* dubbed the dish 'Christmas Pudding' in 1858.

Preparing plum pudding

Many households had their own 'receipt' (recipe) for Christmas pudding, some handed down through families for generations. Most recipes shared a set of common ingredients: finely chopped suet, currants, raisins, and other dried fruit, eggs, flour, milk, spices and brandy. These were mixed together, wrapped in a pudding cloth and boiled four or five hours.

To enhance their flavor after cooking, Christmas puddings hung on hooks to dry out for weeks prior to serving. Once dried, wrapped in alcohol-soaked cheese cloth and placed in earthenware, cooks took the puddings somewhere cool to further age. Some added more alcohol during this period and sealed the puddings with suet or wax to aid in preservation.

Plum pudding traditions

With a food so many centuries in the making, it is not surprising that many traditions have evolved around the preparation and eating of plum pudding.

The last Sunday before Advent, falling sometime between November 20th and 26th, was considered the last day to make Christmas puddings and still give them time to age properly.

It received the moniker 'Stir-up Sunday' because the opening words of the main prayer in the Book of Common Prayer of 1549 for that day are:

"Stir-up, we beseech thee, O Lord, the wills of thy faithful people; that they, plenteously bringing forth the fruit of good works, may of thee be plenteously rewarded; through Jesus Christ our Lord. Amen."

Choir boys parodied the prayer:

"Stir up, we beseech thee, the pudding in the pot. And when we do get home tonight, we'll eat it up hot."

Tradition decrees Christmas pudding be made with thirteen ingredients to represent Christ and the twelve apostles. All family members helped in 'stirring up' the pudding with a special wooden spoon (in honor of Christ's crib.) The stirring had to be done clockwise, from east to west to honor the journey of the Magi, with eyes shut, while making a secret wish.

Some added tiny charms to the pudding. These revealed their finders' fortune. The trinkets often included a thimble for spinsterhood or thrift, a ring for marriage, a coin for wealth, a miniature horseshoe or a tiny wishbone for good luck, a shoe for travel, and an anchor for safe harbor.

At the end of the Christmas feast, the pudding made a dramatic entrance to the dining room. With a sprig of holly on top as a reminder of Jesus' Crown of Thorns and bathed in flaming brandy, representing the Passion of Christ and Jesus' love and power, the Christmas pudding leant a theatrical aspect to the celebration.

Why is it called plum pudding?

And the answer to the most burning question: Why call it 'plum pudding' when it contains no plums?

Dried plums, or prunes, were popular in pies in medieval times, but in the 16th and 17th centuries raisins replaced them. In the 17th century, plums referred to raisins or other dried fruits. The dishes made with them retain the term 'plum' to this day.

Holiday Entertaining

Holiday entertaining began around St. Nicholas Day and extended to Twelfth Night. Small social gatherings, dinner parties, house parties, masquerades, balls, and home theatricals filled the intervening weeks.

In some homes even the servants might be permitted their own festivities, so long as they did not interfere with their employers' plans.

House Parties

Large estates and smaller establishments alike welcomed guests for the Christmastide season. Since travel was difficult and expensive, stays were usually measured in weeks, not days.

Guests did not expect their hosts to entertain them every moment of their stay. They often enjoyed the amenities of the estate on their own.

During the day, gentlemen of the party might form

hunting, fishing or shooting parties, play billiards, chess or cards, ride the grounds of the estate, and indulge in manly conversation discussing topics not appropriate in mixed company, like politics and business. The ladies shared news, patterns and recipes and flaunted their accomplishments to one another. Oftentimes children did not travel with their parents and stayed home with their governess while their parents enjoyed their trip.

Evenings would be spent in mixed company, in the parlor or drawing room, enjoying parlor games, cards, music, conversation and possibly even a little impromptu dancing.

Home theatricals, quite the rage among genteel society who found the increasingly vulgar nature of the theater disturbing, might add additional spice to the house party. On the whole, the activity was well received and even encouraged as a means of entertainment. However, depending on the play chosen, certain elements might disquiet actors and audience alike. Under the guise of the theater, participants might engage in flirtatious and even low, inappropriate behaviors, creating potential moral dilemmas. It behooved the hostess to encourage a prudent choice of theatrical material.

Depending on the weather, hostesses also scheduled outings, picnics, games like pall mall, or skating parties for her guests. Dinner parties, card parties, routs or even a ball brought neighbors in to mix and mingle with the house party guests.

House parties provided an excellent opportunity for young people of equal social status to meet and even a little match-making to occur. A bit of romance added interest and intrigue to a house party and might even result in a wedding later in the season.

Dinner and Dinner Parties

Whether simply a family dinner, or an affair with invited guests, the main meal of the evening was an event unto itself replete with established rules and expectations.

Dressing for dinner

Members of the gentry and upper classes dressed for dinner. Typically dinner required half dress, a semi-formal style worn from afternoon to early evening. Suitably formal manners at the dining table also prevailed.

Most regarded punctuality as a mark of good breeding, so a well-mannered guest arrived for dinner a quarter of an hour before the appointed time. The company assembled in the drawing room to wait for dinner.

John Bell,. *Fashion Plate (French Dinner Party Dress).*

Entry into dining room

Once all the guests arrived and dinner was announced, the company proceeded to the dining room

Early in the Regency period, the ladies entered the dining room first, without the men. The mistress of the house assembled the ladies by ranks. The highest ranking lady led the rest, in order of precedence, into the dining room. The hostess brought up the rear of the company. Once the ladies had taken their seats, the gentlemen followed in the same manner.

Everyone knew the established order of precedence: aristocracy, titled commoners (baronets and knights) and their offspring, married women then single women, in order of seniority.

 n the latter part of the era, etiquette dictated that each gentleman should offer an arm to escort a lady into the dining room. The host always escorted the female guest of the highest social position, and the highest ranking male guest escorted the hostess. From there, paired by precedence, the ladies and gentlemen advanced to the dining room. Poor relations and guests of low consequence followed at the end of the procession.

Seating

The hostess did not assign seats in the dining room. She sat at the head of the table with the ranking male guest at her right. The host took the foot of the table with the ranking female guest at his right. Other guests selected their own seats as they chose, understanding that seats closest to the hostess should be taken by the highest ranking guests.

Later conventions suggested males and females alternate around the table. As a general rule, husbands and wives did not sit together. One saw enough of one's spouse at home and ought to mingle with others on social occasions.

Dinner

Dinner was an elaborate affair, encompassing several courses with a multitude of dishes at each. Many hostesses relished the opportunity to be remembered for her display of wealth and hospitality, offering her guests soup, meat, game, pickles, jellies, vegetables, custards, puddings—anywhere from five to twenty five dishes depending on the grandeur of the occasion. Hostesses who wanted to be especially well remembered might offer a themed meal or one that featured unique and unusual dishes.

Dinner a la Francais

The meal might be served a la Francais, French style, which resembled a modern family style meal. Multiple dishes were presented on the table at the same time. To keep her guests from being overwhelmed by their choices, the hostess acquainted them with all the dishes presented before them.

Each gentleman served himself and the ladies near him from the dishes within his reach. If a dish was required from another part of the table, a manservant would be sent to fetch it. One did not ask a neighbor to pass a dish nor did ladies help themselves.

Gentlemen also poured wine for the ladies near them. If any of the company seem slow in asking for wine, the host would invite them to drink, lest he be thought to begrudge his liquor.

The first course always included soup and fish, often, more than one choice for each. The hostess served the soup, the host, the fish. He also carved all the meat joints.

The first course included a variety of meat, poultry, vegetables, and 'made dishes'. In order to accommodate more dishes than the table could physically hold, courses might include a 'remove.' Half-way through the course, one item would be replaced with another delicacy.

At the end of the course, servants cleared away the dishes and first tablecloth while the diners remained in their seats and enjoyed conversation. They reset the table with a fresh tablecloth and a second course, similar to, but somewhat lighter than the first. At the end of the second course, they cleared the table once more in preparation for the dessert course. Dessert included fruits, nuts, candies, biscuits and little cakes, sweetmeats, blancmange and even ice creams.

Fortunately, guests were not expected to try every dish on the table.

Dinner a la Russe

Hostesses of the 19th century might opt to serve their guests in the Russian style, resembling a modern plated dinner.

Once guests were seated, servants brought out individually plated courses—on average fourteen in total—at roughly ten minute intervals. Courses were plentiful, but small. Each course required its own flatware and wineglass making the place settings for such a dinner formidable.

Toasts

Etiquette required toasts to honor every guest at a dinner party, especially the highest ranking or guest of honor. Failure to toast one's guests suggested no one present was worthy of the honor.

The host made the first toast of the evening, usually in honor of the ranking guest. The toast would honor the guest, preferably in a memorable way, though not a humorous one as that would have been insulting.

To make a toast, a person stood and looked the honoree in the eye, uttered the toast and offered a small, silent bow at the end. Other guests stood for the toast, raised their glasses and drank.

Etiquette experts recommended taking small sips with each toast, especially if the party were large and many toasts likely to occur. Overindulgence was considered ill mannered, but only a very rude guest refused to participate in a toast.

Table manners

During the meal, eating quickly (which inferred poverty) or very slowly (which inferred dislike of the food) was considered vulgar. Those who showed too much interest in their food or were overly finicky about it opened themselves to criticism.

The soup course could never be refused, even if the diner only toyed with it until the fish course. If one ate the soup, it must be scooped with the spoon away from the diner and sipped from the side of the spoon, not the point. Sipping should be accomplished noiselessly—one could not eat too quietly.

Diners must not eat with their nose in the plate nor bring food to her mouth with a knife. If food had any liquid, it should be sopped with the bread and then raised it to the mouth.

A lady's napkin belonged in her lap, a gentlemen's tucked in his collar. Between courses, water in finger bowls allowed hands to be washed as fingers were probably used as frequently as forks.

During dinner, one did not scratch any part of the body, spit, lean elbows on the table, sit too far from the table, or pick teeth before the dishes were removed. A guest did not leave the table before grace was said.

Conversation

During dinner, a gentleman entertained the ladies nearest him with engaging conversation. It was not polite to talk behind one guest's back to another, less so to shout down the table. During the first course, the conversation flowed to the hostesses' left. When the second course was set, the hostess turned to the guest on her right, thus "turning the table" and conversation flowed to her right.

The list of unacceptable topics far outnumbered the acceptable ones. A polite individual did not ask direct personal questions of someone they had just met. To question or even compliment anyone else on the details of their dress might be regarded as impertinent. Scandal and gossip should be omitted from public conversation. Genteel company avoided references to pregnancy, childbirth, or other natural bodily functions. A man could sometimes discuss his hunters or driving horses in the presence of ladies, though it was generally discouraged.

Withdrawing

After dessert, the hostess led the ladies to the drawing room for some time of sex-segregated interaction. When she rose from the table, the other ladies followed her out, in rank order. Without the gentlemen, the ladies enjoyed polite conversation, performed on the piano, or played games.

After the ladies departed, the host produced a decanter of port and perhaps cigars. The men drank, talked about subjects like politics or even introduced salacious topics and jokes, something strictly forbidden in the presence of ladies. After an hour or so, they would rejoin the ladies for parlor games, music and amusements.

Card Parties

Many enjoyed card parties as a way of spending an evening at home with a few friends. They also permitted a budget conscious hostess a way to return social obligations without the expense of a dinner party or a ball. Generally held after dinner, card parties were considered formal, full dress events.

Refreshments
Since the parties occurred late in the evening, guests did not require a full meal. Refreshments were provided, either in the form of light snacks and finger foods brought around by waiters, or by a light supper or tea placed on the sideboards where the guests served themselves. Wine and sherry, for the ladies, and port for the gentlemen would also be provided.

Card Games
Drawing rooms would be set with card tables, candles for each table, and if the budget allowed, new

packs of cards.

Cards in Jane Austen's day lacked the corner indexes of modern cards and had plain, usually white, backs. Stray marks and smudges on the card back could permit cheating, intentional or not. Since most games involved an element of gambling, clean, or better, new cards were very desirable and one way the wealthy could flaunt their means.

Gaming markers, called 'fish' were used to place and collect bets. Stakes could range from pennies upward to staggering amounts.

Games played varied according to the tastes of the guests. These included:

> *Casino,* a game played with two to four players. The goal is to capture cards from the table and score the most points with their captured cards.

> *Commerce* which is played with three to twelve players, who trade or buy cards to achieve the best three-card hand.

> *Cribbage* is a two player game that uses a peg board to keep track of score.

> *Loo* is played with five or more players, who try to take tricks to get a share of the pool.

> *Lottery* is a simple game of chance. The winning player is the one who ends up holding a designated card.

> *Piquet* is a game for two players who create card groups to earn points. The first player to score one hundred points wins.

> *Quadrille* is a complex, four player, trick-taking game.

➢ *Speculation* is played with two to nine players who seek to be the holder of the highest trump card at the end of the round.

➢ *Vingt-un or Pontoon,* is a game for five to eight who seek to have the hand coming closest to a total of twenty-one at the end of the round.

➢ *Whist,* a precursor to today's game of *Bridge,* is a trick-taking game for 4 players in part-nered teams.

Not all guests might be able to afford even small losses at cards. So, a sensitive hostess always provided additional seating in the drawing room for those who might choose to sit out the play. The host and hostess rarely played cards at their own party, leaving them available to make conversation with non-playing guests.

Balls

A Twelfth Night Ball stood out as the highlight event of the Christmastide season. Depending on the hostess, it might be a full dress ball, an 'undress' or 'fancy dress' ball which required costumes, or even a 'Children's Ball' or 'Family Ball' that included the children of the invitees.

Hosting a ball

Hosting a ball meant an enormous amount of work for the hostess and her staff. Cards or invita-tions were sent out no less than two to three weeks (and sometimes as many as six weeks) prior to the event and a reply was imperative within a day or two of receipt. After the ball, thank you notes were expected of all the guests in appreciation for the hospitality.

The entire house would be thrown into disarray in anticipation of the ball. Rooms designated for dancing were emptied of furniture and carpets. The servants, or possibly specially hired artists, chalked the floor with colorful designs to prevent dancers slipping on the smooth floorboards. Space and lightening for the hired musicians were prepared. Chandeliers and additional candles would be added to make the rooms bright and floral arrangements brought in for color and elegance.

Guest rooms had to be readied to accommodate guests who had traveled long distances to the ball or those who had come on foot but became too inebriated to safely return home. A card room, a retiring room for the ladies and the dining room also had to be prepared and staffed.

Balls usually began at ten o'clock in the evening. Supper would be served at half-past twelve or at one o'clock, though small delicacies might have been circulated earlier in the evening. Cooking for the event began days in advance with the hostess overseeing all the particulars.

Opening the ball

Once the guests arrived and were greeted by the hostess, she, the lady of highest rank or the guest of honor took the top position of the first dance and opened the ball. The top lady would 'call the dance', determining the figures, steps and music to be danced. Polite young ladies were cautioned that if they should lead a dance they should not make the figures too difficult for the other dancers, especially if there were younger dancers present.

Dance Partners

Every dance required a partner. At a private ball, unlike a public assembly, everyone was considered introduced, so any young man could ask any young woman to dance. A lady signaled she was interested in dancing by pinning up the train of her gown. If asked to dance, she could not refuse unless she did not intend to dance for the rest of the night.

A young woman did not dance more than two pairs of dances with the same man or her reputation would be at risk. Even two dances signaled to observers that the gentleman in question had a particular interest in her.

Pairs of dances usually lasted half an hour, so an undesirable dance partner could have been quite a burden, especially considering dancing in a large set involved a lot of standing around waiting one's turn to dance. However, if one's partner were pleasing company, it was possible to have private conversations under cover of the crowd.

Gentlemen, unless they retired to the card room, were expected to engage a variety of partners throughout the evening. Failing to do so was an affront to all the guests.

Oftentimes, women outnumbered men at these affairs despite etiquette books warning hostesses to balance their guest lists or better, invite more men than ladies. As a result, it was not uncommon for women to dance with other women rather than sit out the entire evening.

Supper

Halfway through the evening, dancers would pause to refresh themselves with a meal that typically included white soup and negus. One's dance partner for the dance immediately preceding the meal, dubbed the 'supper dance,' usually would be one's dining partner for the meal as well, affording a couple extra time to spend together.

Dances

Supper was quite necessary as most of the dances were lively and bouncy. Country dances, the scotch reel, cotillion, and quadrille made up most of the dancing. Many versions of these dances existed. The lady of the leading couple selected the specific one to be danced. A dance master or master of ceremonies might assist dancers by 'calling the dance' as the musicians played.

In the *country dance,* a line of at least five couples progressed up and down the set in various figures as dancers swung from partner to partner. As they reached the top, each couple would dance down in turn until the entire set had returned to its original positions. In large sets, this could take an hour to complete.

~Rowlandson, 1970

Some insisted that *reels* were better suited to private balls than public assemblies because of their merry character. In this dance four, or sometimes six, dancers would perform interlacing figures with one another then pause for a sequence of fancy footwork similar to a Highland Fling.

The *cotillion* was a French import, with elaborate footwork. Performed in a square or line, like the country dance, it consisted of a "chorus" figure unique to each dance which alternated with a standard series of up to ten "changes" (simple figures such as a right hand star) common to cotillions in general. Some considered cotillions out of fashion by 1800.

The *quadrille* was a shorter dance for four couples arranged in a square, performed to music adapted from popular songs and stage productions. It consisted of five distinct parts or figures assembled from individual cotillions.

By the end of the evening, dancers, especially those who danced every set, would be exhausted. Dancing shoes might be utterly worn through and even gowns in need of repair should an unlucky train have been trod upon. Ices were often served late in the evening to help the dancers cool down from their lively activities.

Christmastide Charity

Amidst all the fun and frivolity of the season, kindness and charity to those in need also figured highly in people's minds. In addition to the normal parish collections and charity baskets for orphanages and neighborhood families, a number of additional seasonal opportunities for charity presented themselves.

St. Thomas' Day

Elderly women and widows went 'thomasing' (also called 'a-gooding') at the houses of their more fortunate neighbors on December 21st, the Feast of St. Thomas the Apostle, hoping for gifts of food or money. The long-standing practice had become even more common since the Napoleonic wars dramatically increased the number of English widows.

'Mumpers' would call at the principle houses in the parish and collect small coins or provisions toward

Christmas dinner for their families. They often carried two-handled pots in which they received gifts of cooked wheat—a very expensive commodity—to make puddings.

In exchange, they offered small gifts of holly sprigs, mistletoe, or handspun yarn and grateful good wishes to their benefactors.

Robert Chambers' Book of Days notes: at Harrington, in Worcestershire, on St. Thomas's Day children went around the village begging for apples, and singing: 'Wassail, wassail, through the town, If you've got any apples, throw them down; Up with the stocking, and down with the shoe, If you've got no apples, money will do; The jug is white and the ale is brown. This is the best house in the town.'

Mummers Plays

A more elaborate form of begging came in the form of the Mummers Play. Actors traversed the streets, asking at nearly every door if mummers were desired there. If so, the outrageously clad actors performed in the streets and squares.

Anti-mask laws prohibited anything that would completely disguise the actors. So, instead of masks, they blackened their faces and decorated their hats and garments with bright ribbons, painted paper and spangles, creating distinct and outrageous costumes. They carried wooden swords and other necessary props to define their characters.

The main players, usually St. George and a soldier often called Slasher, introduced themselves with wild braggadocio before they began their battle. But victory over the forces of evil did not come easily. Before vanquishing his foe, St George would often fall. But

Dr. Quack would appear to restore him to health while the good doctor pontificated on his own medical genius.

After the main act, minor characters would come on the scene to provide irreverent comedy. These characters often included a musical, dancing fool, a poor man concerned with his family, and another with a club and frying pan. The money collector, Devil Doubt, encouraged the audience to contribute to members of the troop who passed among them collecting contributions.

A PARTY OF MUMMERS.
~ Robert Chambers, *Book of Day*

Morris Teams and Sword Dancers

Like Mummers, morris teams of folk dancers and sword dancers performed in the streets and collected donations. Morris men executed rhythmic stepping and highly choreographed figures, sometimes with the aid of implements such as sticks, handkerchiefs and swords. Dancers might blacken their faces, have one member dressed as a woman, and rattle bones or bells as part of their performance.

Some regarded the sword dance as a type of morris, but many regarded it as a separate tradition all together. In it, sword dancers portrayed a stylized representation of combat.

Though many variations of the sword dance existed, they all featured an intricate star maneuver in which the dancers interlocked their swords into a large, multi-pointed star. The sword lock would be placed around one dancer's neck while the dancers circled around their 'victim'. The performance culminated with the feigned beheading of their 'victim' and his miraculous rebirth, symbolizing the cycle of winter's death and spring's rebirth. After the dance, the team members solicited contributions.

s

Caroling

Singing door to door dates back to the time of Shakespeare. Groups of lower class men sang from house to house and remained in rowdy, boisterous groups until someone paid them for their efforts, or simply to leave the premises.

By the end of the 18th century, caroling became less about outright begging and more about charity. Groups of working class men and women went house to house, looking for those with a candle in the window to signal a welcome. When welcomed, they would sing and often receive coins, wassail, and food for their efforts.

During the Regency period, groups of carolers from the local village often ended their evening of caroling at the local land owner's manor house. Typically, they would sing for the family and be treated to victuals and libations (frequently in the form of punch or wassail) and a warm fire.

Start of Caroling

People have celebrated with songs and music since before recorded history. The word 'carol' comes from Latin words meaning *sing* and *joy*. Thus, carols are songs of joy, having origins in both sacred and secular traditions.

Some began as hymns of the church. *Da, puer, plectrum* (Of the Father's Love Begotten), written in the 3rd century by Aurelius Prudentius, is thought to be the oldest documented Christmas carol. Sacred carols continued to be written and sung throughout the Middle Ages. A chaplain in Shropshire noted twenty-five 'caroles of Christmas' in 1426.

Secular celebratory carols have an even longer history, well established in the British Isles by the time of Christianity. Ancient rites marking the arrival of each new season incorporated these songs. These rituals became integrated into observances of Michaelmas, Christmas, Easter and Mid-Summer Day.

By the 17th century though, carols fell out of favor for celebrations other than Christmas. Many of the songs retained their secular, even profane and sacrilegious nature. Consequently, Cromwell found their character so objectionable that he forbade carols when he banned the celebration of Christmas.

Charles II's mid-17th century restoration re-embraced carol singing. By the 18th century, the lyrics of Christmas carols became more decorous and genteel. So much so, they even became popular among the upper classes. Families sang carols in their homes, and churches included religious-themed carols in services.

In some villages, people joined together to sing carols from the church towers. Sellers provided broad-sheets of the most popular carols to assist in the singing. At times, these public celebrations could become boisterous.

CAROL SINGERS OF THE OLDEN TIME.

~Peter Parley, *Tales about Christmas*

What carols might have been sung

Carols sung during Jane Austen's era included both secular and sacred songs.

Some of the secular songs are still familiar today, including: *Deck the Halls, Here We Come a-Wassailing, We Wish you a Merry Christmas* and *The Twelve Days of Christmas*.

Carol hymns that might be familiar to today's carol singers include: *While Shepherds Watched Their Flocks at Night* (1702), *Adestes Fideles/O Come All Ye Faithful* (1760), *Joy to the World* (words, 1719/melody, 1836),

Hark the Herald Angels Sing (1739/1840), *Angels from the Realms of Glory* (1816/1867.)

Older hymns include: *The First Noel,* a traditional Cornish carol which dates from the 18th century and both *God Rest Ye Merry, Gentlemen* and *I Saw Three Ships Come Sailing In,* whose lyrics are found in 17th century texts.

A song book, *Ancient Christmas Carols with the Tunes to which they were formerly sung in the West of England (1822),* offers additional suggestions for the carols Jane Austen might have enjoyed.

The text includes both lyrics and music for:

> ➤ The Lord at first did Adam make
> ➤ When God at first created man
> ➤ A Virgin most pure
> ➤ When righteous Joseph wedded was
> ➤ Hark! Hark! what news the Angels bring
> ➤ Whilst shepherds watched their flocks by night
> ➤ God's Son without beginning
> ➤ Let All that be to Mirth inclined

✤Decorations and Holiday Lights

Families put up decorations and greenery throughout the house on Christmas Eve. Traditional greenery
included holly, ivy, rosemary, evergreen, hawthorn,
laurel, and hellebore (Christmas rose). Boughs, gar-
lands and sprigs decorated windows, tables, mantles
and stairways with the scents and colors of the season. For those who could not go out and cut their
own, greenery could be purchased for the season.

Some households fashioned kissing boughs from
evergreens and mistletoe, adding apples and pretty
ribbon bows for decoration. Young men might 'steal'
a kiss beneath the kissing bow and pluck a mistletoe
berry for each stolen kiss. Oftentimes though, the
mistress of the house relegated these particular decorations below stairs, inappropriate for proper company.

The greenery remained in place until Twelfth Night when it was removed and burned lest it bring bad luck to the house.

DONKEY CART WITH EVERGREENS.

~Peter Parley, *Tales about Christmas*

The Question of Regency Christmas trees

Would Jane Austen have had a Christmas tree? Possibly, but not likely.

The royal family had Christmas trees as early as 1800. Non-royal families with German connections were the most likely commoners to have Christmas trees prior to the mid-1800's. For the rest of the country, Christmas trees only became popular after *The Illustrated London News* published a picture of Victoria and Albert with a family Christmas tree in 1848.

Yule Log

The enormous, freshly cut Yule log arrived at the manor's amidst great ceremony and merriment.

Hauled by teams of farmhands to the hearth, the family would anoint it with oil, salt and wine, and make suitable prayers prior to lighting it.

On Christmas Eve the Yule log would be lit with splinters saved from the previous year's log. The flames consumed personal faults, mistakes and bad choices, allowing everyone in the house to start the year with a clean slate.

The fire was supposed to last until the end of Christmas Day, at least, and keep smoldering until Twelfth Night. If the Yule fire extinguished too early, the house would face bad luck. More ominous, if it cast a headless shadow, that person would die in the new year.

Tradition declared the Yule Log brought prosperity and protection from evil. Families kept a remnant of the log all year so the protection remained across the seasons. Even the ashes protected the house from lightning strikes and the power of the devil. Those who believe in their power scattered the ashes over fields, mixed them into livestock feed to promote fertility, and added them to wells to assure good water.

Christmas or Yule Candle

At the end of the 18th century, chandlers and other merchants often presented regular customers with a large candle at Christmas. The price of candles made it a very generous gift, far more so than it would seem today. This large candle would be lit at sunset on Christmas Eve and burn until Christmas service (or dawn) the next day.

The head of the household placed the Yule Candle on the dining table and lit it at sunset. Once lit, it could not be moved nor any other candle lit from its flame. If it needed to be extinguished, the one who lit it must be the one to perform the service by snuffing, not blowing it out.

Traditional superstitions said that dire consequences, ill fortune or even the death of a family member, would ensue should the candle burn out too soon.

Christmas Eve supper was served in the light of the Yule Candle, which represented Christ as the Light of the World. To prevent bad luck, an even number of people had to sit down to the meal and all leave at the same time after the meal ended. Servants might be pressed to join the family at the table to ensure the desirable even number of diners.

Tradition said the light of the Yule Candle conveyed special blessings to anyone it touched. Cooks stacked holiday breads around it, so they would be kept fresh by its light. Precious possessions might also be placed within its glow to protect them from harm.

The stub of the Yule Candle and its drippings offered protection and healing. The wax might be used on cuts and sores or to mark the backs of farm animals to ensure their health and productivity in the coming year.

❦ A Christmas Feast

Young and old alike anticipated the Christmas feast, and the ensuing celebration that would often include many guests. Hostesses prepared a wide variety of dishes, depending on the tastes and budget of the family, but a few dishes were particularly favored and iconic for the season.

Meat Dishes

Roast beef and Yorkshire pudding were mainstays of a Christmas dinner, but a typical Regency era dinner menu sported multiple meat dishes. Cookery books of the period suggested boar's head, brawn and roast goose as complementary choices for the Christmas meal.

Boar's Head and Brawn

Roasted boar's head often took center stage in the Christmas feast, making a dramatic entrance to the dining room on a platter with an apple stuffed in its mouth.

People deeply feared wild boars, though they became extinct in England during the 17th century. Boar as a main dish at a meal represented the victory of good over evil. In the 18th century, a pig's head substituted for the wild boar.

Brawn was another pork-based Christmas treat. Recipes for it are reminiscent of modern headcheese featuring ox feet and pork belly boiled, chilled and sauced.

Christmas Goose

For most of the 19th century, goose occupied a place of honor at Christmas dinner. Though not difficult to prepare, the bird's size often posed challenges for modest kitchens. Local bakers provided a solution, roasting birds for customers to pick up on their way home from church on Christmas day. Apparently 'take out' food is not a new idea.

Sometimes, cooks made a Yorkshire Christmas pie with the goose. The dish resembled a modern turducken (turkey stuffed with duck stuffed with chicken). The pie called for a turkey, a goose, a fowl, a partridge, and a pigeon, cooked boned, seasoned, and stuffed into each other, then wrapped inside a generous pastry crust and baked. Families often sent these to friends and relatives as the thick crusts enabled them to travel well.

Mince Meat Pie

Most considered mince meat pies, also known as Christmas or Twelfth Night pies, Christmas feast staples.

These pies trace back to the 13th century when crusaders returned with Middle Eastern recipes that featured meat, fruit and spices. Mixing meat with fruit and spices helped preserve the meat without smoke, drying or salt.

In the 15th century, King Henry V served a mincemeat pie at his coronation. His descendent, King Henry VIII preferred his Christmas pie as a main-dish pie more savory than sweet.

Originally, the mince pies were oblong or oval. In that shape, the pastry crust tended to sink in the middle, resembling Jesus' manger. Sometimes, bakers made a small doll from pastry, placed it in the center and called them 'crib pies'.

During the 1600's, the pies became circular, though they might be as large as 20 lbs. In the intervening centuries, they became smaller.

Not all appreciate the indulgent treats, though. Puritans frowned on rich food and alcoholic drink. Minced pies represented both and were not considered fit to occupy a clergyman's plate.

During Cromwell's rule as Lord Protector in the mid-1600's, his council banned the celebration of Christmas. Though mince pies were never actually made illegal, they were frowned upon. A 1656 satire called 'Christmas Day' calls them 'Idolatrie in a Crust'. Following Cromwell's death, though, Christmas celebrations and minced pie returned in force.

Recipes varied by region, but usually included: beef and other meats, suet, sugar, fruits, spices, citrus peel, eggs and brandy; many of the same ingredients found in plum pudding. Leftovers from the Christmas feast might be used to make pies for the twelve days until Epiphany. Pies could be made up shortly after the feast and last up to two months in cool weather.

When making the minced-meat filling, custom said it should be stirred only clockwise; counterclockwise stirring would bring bad luck for the coming year. Moreover, the filling should include cinnamon, cloves and nutmeg to represent the gifts of the Magi to the infant Jesus, and a star shaped bit of pastry should top the pie for the star of Bethlehem.

Eating minced pie all twelve days of Christmas would bring twelve months of happiness in the new year. To strengthen the charm, the pies must be baked by the dozen and offered by friends, but the pies should be eaten in silence.

Sweet Dishes

Sweets also played a role on the Christmas table, though they might not be served as a separate course. Towering jellies molded in fancy shapes might be placed alongside fish and poultry. Almond paste (marzipan), sugar cakes (shortbread), trifles, rice puddings and apple dumplings often appeared among dishes brought out for the second course of the meal.

Black Butter

Jane Austen mentioned black butter in one of her letters. Containing no butter at all, it resembled apple butter of today. Various recipes included different fruits, along with sugar, lemon and spices. These were cooked over long periods to reduce the fruit to a dark colored, sweet spread.

Fruit Cake

Decadent fruit cakes appeared for special occasions like Christmas. As with the yule log and yule candle, saving a portion of the holiday fruit cake for the following year brought good luck. The quantities of alcohol and dried fruit in the cake made it quite possible for it to last that long.

Another perennial favorite, gingerbread often appeared with the Christmas pudding at the end of the meal.

Beverages

Not only did special dishes appear on the table for the holidays, but special beverages graced the sideboards as well.

Wassail and Punch

Punch, a traditional drink for company, usually contained large amounts of alcohol. Prior to the 19th century, drinkers shared from a communal punch bowl, usually made of imported ceramics. During the Regency era, smaller, individual punch cups, served from the larger bowl, replaced the communal vessel.

Though the recipes varied, they generally included spirits (rum, brandy, and port), fruit juice, citrus peels and sugar. Wassail, a close cousin to punch, contained apple cider, spice, sugar, rum and brandy, and would be served hot.

Full of expensive ingredients and time consuming to prepare, due to hand peeling, squeezing and sieving fruits, punch was certainly not a drink for children and could, in large quantities, easily lead to riotous behavior.

Syllabub
Syllabub also took several forms, but in all preparations it contained a mixture of alcohol, cream, sugar and citrus, and was somewhat less potent than egg nog. Some recipes called for making it nearly solid, even dried for a day before consuming. Other recipes suggested preparing it directly under the milk-cow. No matter the recipe, like punch, syllabub was relatively expensive and reserved for special occasions.

All the period recipes in this chapter are collected in this book's final chapter: A Great Deal of Good Food.

.

Gift Giving

Though gift giving did not occupy the forefront of the Christmastide season, people did give gifts. St. Nicholas Day, Christmas Day and Twelfth Night were the most likely days for gift exchange, although old traditions called for gifts to be presented on New Year's Day.

Custom required certain gifts of obligation between unequal parties. Land owners and the well-off presented charitable gifts to beggars and the poor of the community. They also provided favors to their tenants, servants and the tradesmen they patronized. These tokens might be coins, food, particularly expensive foodstuffs, or cast-off clothes and goods.

Gifts might also be presented from those lower in status to those above them. Beggars offered songs, holly sprigs or simple handicrafts to their benefactors. Tradesmen sent special goods like Yule candles to their best patrons. Tenants might bestow gifts of their harvest to the landowner in recognition of his generosity and possibly to encourage him not to raise their rents.

Social equals like friends and family also indulged in gift giving, though men and women did not exchange gifts unless they were married, engaged or related by blood. These gifts tended to be far more thoughtful and personal than obligatory gifts.

Ladies often gave items that showcased both their accomplishments and the tastes of the recipient. Skilled hands prepared embroidered handkerchiefs, slippers and other fine accessories for loved ones. Clever needles could create scarves, shawls, laces, trims and similar items. Paintings, drawings and other decorative arts graced boxes, screens and even small furniture items.

Givers could, and often did purchase gifts, with clothing and jewelry pieces (especially those made with locks of hair) among the most common items for both sexes. Books, sheet music, fancy boxes and supplies for activities like writing or handicrafts enjoyed great popularity as holiday presents.

Gift giving, especially on Christmas day, became more prevalent toward the end of the Regency period and into the Victorian. Advertisers began running ads in periodicals suggesting novel ideas for gifts. One 1814 advertisement in Ackermann's Repository suggested Marston's patent stays and corsets, designed to 'comfortably support the weak and debilitated', would make a most acceptable Christmas gift for one's parents.

❧ Boxing Day

Traditionally a day for fox hunting, the day after Christmas, St. Stephen's Day, also served as an important day for distributing gifts and charity.

Servants often enjoyed a rare day off on Boxing Day. This may not seem like much to modern sensibilities, but servants had very little time off, much less coordinated time off with other family members. The day off on Boxing Day often meant that families could visit together even though they might work at different establishments.

Employers and patrons handed out 'Christmas boxes' containing old clothing and extra items to servants and tradesmen on Boxing Day. Old clothing might not seem like a particularly desirable gift. However, in Jane Austen's day, textiles were very expensive. Only the very wealthy cast off old clothing. Others remade it into other garments by taking them apart, re-cutting and possibly re-dying the fabric.

When clothes could no longer be remade, they were made into cleaning cloths, rags and even rugs. A healthy trade in second-hand garments also existed. So, if the gift's lucky recipient could use neither the garment nor its fabric, it could always be sold.

Landowners and the well-off were expected to be especially generous on Boxing Day. Many held a kind of open house for tenants and less fortunate neighbors, often giving food or money so the needy might celebrate on their own.

Churches collected money in alms-boxes during the season and distributed it to the needy after Christmas, often opening the boxes on Boxing Day.

Rather than marking the end of the holiday season, Boxing Day marked the beginning of festivities like Christmas Pantomimes, which would culminate on Twelfth Night.

BOXING DAY.
~Peter Parley, *Tales about Christmas*

Pantomimes

Each year, theaters prepared Christmas panto-
mimes (pantos) that would begin on Boxing Day and
run as long as the audiences demanded them. These
were not silent productions, but rather very verbal
performances that included the audience as an extra
character in plays bearing many similarities to modern
burlesque.

Most of the pantos merged children's fairy tales or
stories like Robinson Crusoe or Sinbad the Sailor,
with the fantastical star-crossed lovers of the harle-
quinade story. The characters included: Harlequin,
astute jester and romantic hero; Columbine, a fairy-
like love interest for Harlequin; Pantaloon, a silly old
man, father to Columbine; and comic servants, Sprite
and Clown.

~J. L. Marks, *Mr Ellar as Harlequin*

Dual titles, like
'Harlequin and
Cinderella,'
paid homage
to both ele-
ments of the
production.
Typically, the
panto began in
the fairy-story
world with a
cross, business
minded, old
father trying to

force his pretty daughter to marry a wealthy fop despite her preference for another, worthy though poorer, suitor. A good fairy transforms the lovers into the harlequin characters in a spectacular scene of magic followed by the most dramatic part of the production, a frenzied chase scene.

These much anticipated, fast paced scenes included slapstick comedy, dancing and acrobatic displays which helped one of the most famous clowns, Joseph Grimaldi, to lift Clown to one of the most important roles in the show.

While one part of the performance was aimed at the children and the innocent, adults responded to the often risqué or politically charged verbal exchanges. Since the audience participated in the show, emotions could run high. So much so, a pantomime could, and occasionally did, incite a riot..

New Year's Eve

For some, New Year's Eve meant thoroughly cleaning the house to start the new year clean. Old superstitions required ashes, rags, scraps and anything perishable to be removed from the house so that nothing carried over from one year to the next. In this way, the family would preserve their good luck and banished the bad.

Some celebrated with the family or a party gathering in a circle before midnight. At the stroke of the midnight hour, the head of the family would open the front and back doors to usher the old year out the back and welcome the new year in the front.

First Footing

Some Scots and residents of northern England believed the first visitor to set foot across the threshold (the first-footer) after midnight on New Year's Eve affected the family's fortunes. Ladies, in particular, wished for a tall, dark, and handsome male stranger without physical handicap, especially if his feet were the right shape.

High-insteps implied that *water would run under*— that is bad luck would flow past. A flat foot meant bad luck, as did women in most cases. Not all agreed on these omens. For some, blonde or red-headed, bare-foot girls brought good luck.

The first-footer entered through the front door, ideally, bearing traditional gifts: a coin, a lump of coal, a piece of bread or shortbread, whiskey, salt and a black bun—representing financial prosperity, warmth, food, good cheer, and flavor in the new year. Tradition held that no one spoke until the 'first-footer' wished the occupants a happy new year.

Once inside, the first-footer would be led through the clean home to place the coal on the fire and offer a toast to the house and all who lived there. Then the first-footer might be permitted to kiss every woman in the house. The first-footer would leave through the back door and take all the old year's troubles and sorrows.

Dark haired young men often made the rounds of the neighborhood houses, bringing good luck to the homes and to themselves when invited in for a holiday toast.

New Year's Day

A variety of traditions for New Year's Day suggested how one might discern or influence fortunes for the coming year.

In one, a farmer hooked a large, specially baked pancake on one of a cow's horns. Others gathered about to sing and dance around the unsuspecting bovine and encourage it to toss its head. If the cake fell off in front of the cow, it foretold good luck, if behind, bad.

In Hertfordshire, at sunrise on New Year's Day, farmers burned a hawthorn bush in the fields to ensure good luck and bountiful crops.

Creaming the Well

In some regions, young women raced to draw the first water from the well, a practice known as *'creaming the well.'* Possession of this water meant marriage within the coming year if she could get the man she desired to marry to drink the water before the end of the day.

Others believed the water had curative properties and even washed the udders of cows with it to ensure productivity.

Until the 18th century, gifts of food, money and clothing (especially gloves) were exchanged on New Year's Day instead of Christmas or Twelfth Night.

In Scotland and the northern regions of England, traditional New Year's foods included: shortbread, venison pie, haggis, black bun (similar to mince pie) and rumbledethumps, similar to bubble and squeak or colcannon.

Wassailing

Wassailing and caroling are often used interchangeably as terms for singers going from house to house. But in the Regency era, particularly in cider producing regions, wassailing had a different meaning.

Wassailers might go from door to door, with a large wassail bowl filled with spiced ale. They sang and drank to the health of those they visited. In return, recipients of their blessings gave them drink, money and Christmas food.

On the Twelfth Night or its eve, wassailers also blessed orchards and fields and sometimes even cows. A wassail King and Queen led the singers in a tune as they traversed from one orchard to the next.

In some traditions, the Queen would be lifted into one of the trees, often the largest, where she placed wassail soaked toast as a gift to the tree spirits.

Other customs had the men bless the tree and drink to its health. They would circle the largest tree in the orchard while singing and splashing it with cider. The rest of the group would sing, shout, blow horns, and bang drums or pots, until gunmen fired a volley into the branches in hopes of chasing away evil spirits. Sometimes, fires were lit and tended through the night while the wassailers went to the next orchard.

In Herefordshire, wheat fields were lit with bonfires and wassailed similarly to orchards.

WASSAILING THE COW.
~Peter Parley, *Tales about Christmas*

Twelfth Night

The exciting climax of the Christmastide season came on Epiphany or Twelfth Night (January 5 or 6 depending on who counted.) A time for putting away social norms, and a feast day to mark the coming of the Magi, it was the traditional day to exchange gifts.

Revels, masks and balls filled the day and night. Elaborate and expensive Twelfth Day cakes covered with colored sugar frosting, gilded paper trimmings, and sometimes delicate plaster of Paris or *pastillage* figures made impressive centerpieces for the party. In towns, confectioners displayed these cakes in their shop windows, illuminated by small lamps so their wares could be admired during winter evenings.

Alongside the cakes, revelers might find white soup, mince pies, jellies, and marzipan to be washed down with alcoholic punches. Guests would don costumes and portray outlandish characters during parlor games and dancing, leading to potentially raucous celebrations.

By midnight, decorations had to be taken down and burned or one would face bad luck for the rest of the year. Some believed that for every branch that remained a goblin would appear.

Twelfth Night Characters

Twelfth Night revels frequently involved guests randomly selecting a character to play for the evening by drawing a slip of paper at the start of the party. Some hostesses would send characters assignments around to her guests so that they could come already dressed to play their part. Others might provide dress up items for their guests to don after characters had been chosen. Guests had to remain in character for the entire evening or pay a forfeit.

In addition to the obligatory King and Queen, common characters included Sir Gregory Goose, Sir Tumbelly Clumsy, Miss Fanny Fanciful and Mrs. Candour. Some also included roles from popular literature and plays. Stationers sold sets of pre-made characters, or a hostess might copy them from books on games and merry-making.

Rachel Revel's *Merrymaker's Companion*_offered an extensive set of characters. She recommended that as each character was drawn, the game's conductor arrange them in order of their number and when all the guests had characters, they might each read lines in turn to introduce themselves. For example:

1. King: Fate decrees me your King: grave and gay, wise and fools, Must consent, for this night, to submit to my rules.

2. Queen: I'm your Queen: good my liege, your confessor, may shrive you; But for me, I'm resolved, if I can't lead I'll drive you.

3. Lord Spendthrift: Blood, for money, Lord Spendthrift is ready to barter, if some rich maid will purchase a Knight of the garter.

4. Molly Mumper: Molly Mumper wants a husband: Baron, or Duke, she cares not which; If you'll marry a beggar's heiress, she'll promise to make you rich.

5. Lucy Leerwell: "Tis so humdrum to live single, Lucy Leerwell would prefer, On some facetious youth, her hand and fortune to confer.

6. Joe Giber: Take Joe Giber, the king's jester, he's the fellow for your yoke, Tho' marriage, it must be confess'd, by most wits is counted no joke.

7. Miss All-agog: Miss All-agog's a candid girl, who hates monastic vows, And she will never take the veil if she can get a spouse.

8. Sam Sadboy: Sam Sadboy's neither monk nor friar; he sees into your views: Marry him, you may cast off your veil, and the rest of your deeds when you choose.

9. Miss Romance: Miss Romance to accept for her partner proposes, One who'll print in his press ev'ry work she composes...

The hostess might also have the ladies pick men's names from a hat. The lucky gentlemen would be her partner for the entire evening's festivities.

Fun and Games

A well-chosen parlor game allowed young people to engage in a great deal of harmless fun that might otherwise be considered inappropriate in society at large. A great deal of flirtation might be undertaken in the presence of a chaperone with them being left none the wiser for it.

Word games offered the opportunity to communicate with someone of the opposite sex with openness not otherwise possible. Good humor and frivolity provided an easy front for a more serious purpose.

A game of 'Short Answers' allowed a clever player to ask otherwise inappropriately direct questions to a potential lover. 'I Love my Love with an A' gave players opportunity to bestow compliments not generally considered proper.

Game players did not limit themselves to staid word or memory games. A number of active and even rowdy games graced the pages of game books like Rachel Revel's.

Daring, drama and a gracious acceptance of consequences went hand in hand with playing messy games like bobbing for apples, 'Bullet Pudding' (in which one used their teeth to search a bullet in a pile of flour) and 'Snapdragon' (which featured flaming brandy and a bowl of raisins.)

A young woman's figure or young gentleman's fine calves might be shown to great advantage in a game of 'How d'ye do? How d'ye do?' Even more daring, players scrambled for open chairs in games like 'Move-all' or 'The Toilette' and ran the risk of running into each other or accidently sitting in someone's lap. Under the cover of a parlor game, it was all in good fun, not a source for gossip or scandal.

The end of Twelfth Night Revels

Although Twelfth Night revelry could be peaceable and even family-friendly, the combination of good humor, spirited games and large quantities of highly alcoholic punch often made for riotous festivities.

In the 1870's, Queen Victoria outlawed the celebration of Twelfth Night in fear the parties had become out of control.

~ Snapdragon. Robert Chambers, *Book of Day*

✥ Parlor games

People of all ages and all social classes played parlor games. While competitive spirits drove some players to win, winning was not always desirable. Losers paid forfeits, which could be an elaborate penalty or dare, but more often forfeits served as a thinly disguised machination for getting a kiss. Often, forfeits accumulated all evening, until the hostess would *'cry the forfeits'* and they would all be redeemed.

Rachel Revel's book offers guidelines for various amusements suitable for genteel company in the drawing room. Games Jane Austen might have played during Christmas parties include:

Active Games

When the parlor or drawing room was large enough or a party could go outside, active games added to the merriment. These games could require a great deal of running about and even physical contact between the players. Since etiquette forbade almost all touching between the genders, active games provided a rare opportunity that an enterprising young person could use to their advantage.

Blind man's bluff and its variations

Many variations of this game existed. All included a blindfolded player trying to guess the identity of another player who taps them or whom they have caught. A great deal of cheating was generally involved (and expected,) which only added to the sport.

Buffy Gruffy

blindfolded player stands in the middle of the room. The others arrange their chairs in a circle and silently trade places. The blindfolded player walks around the chairs and stops in front of one and questions the seated player. That player answers while disguising their voice as much as possible, possibly mocking or teasing the blindfolded player in the process.

After three questions and answers, the blindfolded player must guess who they have questioned. If they are correct, the seated player takes the blindfold and play begins anew. Otherwise, the blindfolded player moves on to try again.

Hot Cockles

A variety of Buffy Gruffy. A blindfolded player rests with their head in another player's lap. The other players run up and touch the blindfolded person's shoulder. He/she then tries to guess who tapped them. If correct, the person identified takes the blind-fold and the game starts over.

Move-All
Chairs are arranged in as large a circle as possible. One player stands in the center and calls 'Move all'. Everyone rises and dashes for another chair. The player left without a chair takes the center for the next round.

The Ribbon
One player stands in the center of the room holding ribbons. The remaining players form a circle around the center and each take the loose end of a ribbon. The player in the center then calls '*pull*' or '*let go.*' At the command '*let go*', all the players must pull on their ribbons. At '*pull*' they must let go their ends. The center player calls instructions until one player makes a mistake. Players who make errors pay forfeits.

Steal the White Loaf
A chosen player, 'it', stands with their back to the others and a 'treasure' on the floor behind him/her. Another player tries to sneak up and steal the treasure. If 'it' turns around and sees them moving, then they are 'caught' and become 'it'.

The Toilette
One player takes the role of lord or lady. The rest of the players take on the name of some article of the toilette: comb, curling-irons, powder-puff, mirror, etc.

The lord or lady calls for some article. The player who is that article trades places with the lord or lady and the play continues. If a player does not jump when called or forgets their article, a forfeit is paid.

For variety, the lord or lady may call 'all my toilette' and everyone must jump up, change seats and take the toilette article of the player who had been in that seat. The player remaining without a seat becomes the lord or lady and play continues.

Word/Memory Games

When weather, space, or personal preferences did not favor active games, staid word and memory games allowed for flirtation in quiet ways. Clever players could find ways to convey outrageous messages to one another under cover of a rhyme or required response.

The Doctor

Each player is a patient. The doctor comes, feels the pulse of the first patient, asks after the disorder, and then orders a remedy in contrast to the patient's complaint.

For example, if the patient complains of cold the doctor might order something hot; if the patient is feverish, a basket of snow -balls, two at night, one in the morning; if plagued with a sour stomach, a quart of decoction of sweet-william, with a pound of sugar, every four hours.

After going all round, the doctor addresses any one of the party, and says, "_____ (one of the players) is ill of such a complaint. What would you order in that case?" if the player cannot remember the remedy prescribed, he must pay a forfeit. The next player is asked a similar question, until all the players have been queried.

I Love My Love With An A.

Every person takes a letter and completes the verse with words beginning with that letter. The most difficult letters like X, Y, Z may be left out. Anyone who cannot fulfill their verse or who repeats what has been said by another must pay a forfeit.

This game may be played with a short verse or a long one. The short version: I love my love with an A, because she is ardent: I hate her, because she is ambitious. I took her to Andover, to the sign of the Angel. I treated her with artichokes; and her name is Anne Adair.

The longer version: I love my love with an S, because she is sensible; I hate her, because she is sarcastic; by way of presents, I gave her Shenstone, a squirrel, a sea-gull, and a sensitive plant; I took her to Salisbury, to the sign of the Sun, and treated her with soup, salmon, sand-larks, shaddocks, and sherry; her name is Selina Smith, and she is dressed in sarsnet.

Short Answers

The players are seated in a circle, ladies and gentlemen alternately. A lady asks her right-hand neighbor a question, to which he replies with single syllable words. Longer words will exact a penalty, one for each additional syllable. He then turns to the next lady with a question. The questions may be mundane as in: Pray sir, permit me to ask if you love dancing? Or unique as in: Pray madam, what wood do you think the best for making thumb-screws? Neither question nor answer may be repeated. Any player who repeats a question or answer incurs a forfeit.

Messy Games

If players desired more lively indoor activities, several messy games might suit. These games were not for the faint of heart though, as no one's dignity was likely to survive unscathed.

Bobbing for Apples

The hostess provided a large vessel of water with an appropriate quantity of apples floating in it. Players had to capture an apple from the water using only their teeth.

The thin muslins worn by fashionable young ladies of the era became rather transparent when wet. No doubt this leant a rather tantalizing aspect to the activity.

Bullet pudding

Flour would be piled into a high mound and a bullet placed on the top. Players cut slices out of the flour pile with a knife without dislodging the bullet. If the bullet fell, the player had to retrieve the bullet from the flour with their teeth.

Snapdragon

Raisins would be piled in a bowl, topped with brandy and lit on fire. Players tried to snatch raisins out of the blue brandy-flames and eat them without getting burned—or lighting anything else aflame. The guest with the most raisins was destined to find true love in the upcoming year.

Performance Games

Without television or radio to provide daily doses of drama and comedy, people of Jane Austen's day turned to parlor games to supply amusing performances. Those with a talent for theatrical presentation could find themselves a very popular parlor guest.

Charades

The game could be played two different ways. In one, each player in turn would recite a riddle, and the rest had to guess at their word.

In the second, the party would divide into two or more groups. Each group would create short one minute acts to describe the syllables, the last describing the whole word for the rest of the party to guess.

The Courtiers

The monarch sits in the center of the room and performs a series of moves, simple, humorous or even vulgar, that the courtiers must copy. The first courtier to laugh loses and becomes the next monarch.

How d'ye do? How d'ye do?

The players stand in a circle. The first person begins jumping up and down in the stiffest manner possible, holding their head up high in front of another player, and crying, "How d'ye do, how d'ye do, how d'ye do, how d'ye do?"

The other jumps in the same manner and cries, "Tell me who, tell me who, tell me who, tell me who."

The first person names another of the party, stops jumping, and resumes his place in the circle.

'Tell me who' then jumps up to the person indicated, crying, "How d'ye do?" and the game continues making sure to include every player in the activity.

Hunt the slipper

"Cobblers" sit on the floor. A "customer" hands them a shoe and turns their back. The "cobblers" pass the shoe behind their backs while the "customer" counts to ten. The "customer" turns around and tries to guess who has the shoe. When the correct "cobbler" is identified, the "customer" and "cobbler" trade places and the game starts again.

Musical Magic

One of the party leaves the room until the rest decide what task he will be required to perform. The task might be as simple as snuffing a candle, or as complex as kneeling before another player, removing their ring and placing it on the finger of the other player.

The player is guided in his task by the playing of music from soft to loud. When the player is close to the object or action he must do next, the music becomes louder until it stops when he has gotten it right. The further away the player for the desired action, the softer the music. If the player gives up, a forfeit must be paid and another player takes his place.

A Great Deal of Good Food: Period Recipes

Country house parties, or even large gatherings in the city, required a great deal of food. The mistress of the household and her staff could be kept busy for days, even weeks with holiday preparations.

Without modern conveniences like refrigeration and electric appliances, cooking was an extremely labor intensive process. Fancy holiday foods increased the amount of effort, with some 'receipts' (recipes) taking days to complete. Others called for beating ingredients by hand for thirty or forty minutes at a time, mincing, grating and forcing through sieves, or boiling and stirring for hours. By the end of the season, nerves could wear very thin with all the efforts.

These recipes, mentioned in earlier chapters, are quoted directly from their period sources. Some punctuation has been changed to make them more readable, but all spellings, ingredient names and terms have been left original. Compared to modern recipes, measurements are inexact at best, and cooking directions often leave a great deal to the imagination.

❋ SAVORY DISHES

Meats

Roast Beef.
If beef, be sure to paper the top, and baste it well all the time it is roasting, and throw a handful of salt on it. When you see the smoke draw to the fire, it is near enough; then take off the paper, baste it well, and drudge it with a little flour to make a fine broth.

Never salt your roast meat before you lay it to the fire, for that draws out all the gravy. If you would keep it a few days before you dress it, dry it very well with a clean cloth, then flour it all over, and hang it where the air will come to it; but be sure always to mind that there is- no damp place about it, if there is, you must dry it well with a cloth.

Take up your meat, and garnish your dish with nothing but horse-radish.

~Hannah Glasse

To roast Porker's Head.
Choose a fine young head, clean it well and put bread and sage as for pig; sew it up tight and on a string or hanging jack roast it as a pig, and serve with the same sauce.

~Eliza Rundell

To make Sham Brawn.

Take the belly piece, and head of a young pork, rub it well with salt-petre, let it lie three or four days, wash it clean; boil the head, and take off all the meat, and cut it in pieces, have four neat's feet boiled tender, take out the bones, and cut it in thin slices, and mix it with the head, and lay it in the belly-piece, and roll it up tight, and bind it round with sheet-tin.

Boil it four hours; take it up, and set it on one end, put a trencher on it within the tin, and a large weight upon that, and let it stand all night; in the morning take it out, and bind it with a fillet; put it in spring-water and salt, and it will be fit for use.

When you use it, cut it in slices like brawn. Garnish with parsley. Observe to change the pickle every four or five days, and it will keep a long time.

~*Hannah Glasse*

Directions for roasting a Goose.

Take some sage, wash and pick it clean, and an onion; chop them very fine, with some pepper and salt, and put them into the belly; let your goose be clean picked, and wiped dry with a dry cloth, inside and out; put it down to the fire, and roast it brown: one hour will roast a large goose, three quarters of an hour, a small one. Serve it in your dish with some brown gravy, apple-sauce in a boat, and some gravy in another.

~*Hannah Glasse*

Soups

White Soup.

To six quarts of water put in a knuckle of veal, a large fowl, and a pound of lean bacon, and half a pound of rice, with two anchovies, a few pepper corns, two or three onions, a bundle of sweet herbs, three or four heads of celery in slices, stew all together, till your soup is as strong as you choose it

Then strain it through a hair sieve into a clean earthen pot, let it stand all night, then take off the scum, and pour it clear off into a tossing-pan, put in half a pound of Jordan almonds beat fine, boil it a little and run it through a lawn sieve, then put in a pint of cream and the yolk of an egg. Make it hot, and send it to the table.

~*John Simpson*

To make Mock-Turtle Soup.

Take a calf's head, and scald the hair off as you would a pig, and wash it very clean. Boil it in a large pot of water half an hour; then cut all the skin off by itself, take the tongue out. Take the broth made of a knuckle of veal, put in the tongue and skin, with three large onions, half an ounce of cloves and mace, and half a nutmeg beat fine, all sorts of sweet herbs chopped fine, and three anchovies, stew it till tender.

Then take out the meat, and cut it in pieces about two inches square, and the tongue in slices; mind to skin the tongue; strain the liquor through a sieve; take half a pound of butter, and put in the stew-pan, melt it, and put in a quarter of a pound of flour. Keep it stirring till it is smooth, then put in the liquor; keep it stirring till all is in, if lumpy strain it through a sieve;

then put to your meat a bottle of Madeira wine. Season with pepper and salt, and Cayenne pepper pretty high; put in force-meat balls and egg-balls boiled, the juice of two lemons, stew it one hour gently, and then serve it up in tureens.

N. B. If it is too thick, put some more broth in before you stew it the last time.

~*Hannah Glasse*

Hare soup.

This being a rich soup, is proper for a large entertainment, and may be placed at the bottom of the table, where two soups are required, and almond Or onion soup be at the top. Hare soup is thus made: Cut a large old hare into small pieces, and put it in it mug, with three blades of mace, a little salt, two large onions, a red herring, six morels, half a pint of red wine, and three quarts of water.

Bake it three hours in a quick oven, and then strain it into a tossing-pan. Have ready boiled three ounces of French barley, or sago, in water. Then put the liver of the hare two minutes in scalding water, and rub it through a hair sieve with the back of a wooden spoon; put it into the soup with the barley, or sago, and a quarter of a pound of butter. Set it over the fire, and keep it stirring, but do not let it boil. If you disapprove of the liver, you may put in crisped bread, steeped in red wine.

~John Perkins

Onion Soup.

Boil eight or ten large Spanish onions in milk and water, change it three times. When they are quite soft, rub them through a hair sieve. Cut an old cock in pieces, and boil it for gravy, with one blade of mace. Strain it, and pour it upon the pulp of the onions. Boil it gently with the crumb of an old penny loaf, grated into half a pint of cream; add kyan pepper and salt to your taste. A few heads of asparagus, or boiled spinach, both make it eat well and look very pretty. Grate a crust of brown bread round the edge of the dish.

~John Perkins

Puddings and Pies

A Yorkshire Pudding.

Take a quart of milk and five eggs, beat them up well together, and mix them with flour till it is of a good pancake batter, and very smooth; put in a little salt, some grated nutmeg and ginger; butter a dripping or frying-pan, and put it under a piece of beef, mutton, or a loin of veal, that is roasting, and then put in your batter, and when the top-side is brown, cut it in square pieces, and turn it, and then let the underside be brown. Put it in a hot dish, as clean from fat as you can, and send it to table hot.

~*John Perkins*

To make an Oatmeal Pudding.

TAKE a pint of fine oatmeal, boil it in three pints of new milk, stirring it till it is as thick as a hasty-pudding; take it off, and stir in half a pound of fresh butter, a little beaten mace and nutmeg, and a gill of sack; then beat up eight eggs, half the whites, stir all well together, lay puff-paste all over the dish, pour in the pudding, and bake it half an hour. Or you may boil it with a few currants.

~*Hannah Glasse*

To make a Potato- Pudding.

TAKE a quart of potatoes, boil them soft, peel them, and mash them with the back of a spoon, and rub them through a sieve, to have them fine and smooth *y* take half a pound of fresh butter melted, half a pound of fine sugar, beat them well together till they are very smooth, beat six eggs, whites and all, stir them in, and a glass of sack or brandy. You may add half a pound of currants, boil it half an hour, melt butter with a glass of white wine; sweeten with sugar, and pour over it. You may bake it in a dish, with puff-paste all round the dish at the bottom.
    ~*Hannah Glasse*

To make a common Rice Pudding.

Wash half a pound of rice, put to it three pints of good milk, mix it well with a quarter of a pound of butter, a stick or two of cinnamon beaten fine, half a nutmeg grated, one egg well beat, a little salt and sugar to your taste.

One hour and a half will bake it in a quick oven; when it comes out take off the top, and put the pudding in breakfast cups, turn them into a hot dish like little puddings, and serve it up.
    ~ *Elizabeth Raffald*

A Rice-Pudding baked.

Boil a pound of rice just till it is tender; then drain all the water from it as dry as you can, but do not squeeze it; then stir in a good piece of butter, and sweeten to your palate. Grate a small nutmeg in, stir it all well together, butter a pan, and pour it in and bake it. You may add a few currants for change.

~*Hannah Glasse*

Note: In the following pie recipes, 'paste' refers to pastry crust dough.

A Venison Pasty.

Take a neck and breast of venison, bone them, and season them well with pepper and salt, put them into a deep pan, with the best part of a neck of mutton sliced and laid over them. Pour in a glass of red wine, put a coarse paste over it, and bake it two hours in an oven.

Then lay the venison in a dish, and pour the gravy over it, and put one pound of butter over it; make a good puff-paste, and lay it near half an inch thick round the edge of the dish roll out the lid, which must be a little thicker than the paste on the edge of the dish, and lay it on. Then roll out another lid pretty thin, and cut in flowers, leaves, or whatever form you please, and lay it on the lid.

If you do not want it, it will keep in the pot that it was baked in eight or ten days; but let the crust be kept on that the air may not get to it. A breast and a shoulder of venison are most proper for a pasty.

~*John Perkins*

To make a Yorkshire Christmas-Pie.

First make a good standing crust, let the wall and bottom be very thick; bone a turkey, a goose, a fowl, a partridge, and a pigeon, Season them all very well, take half an ounce of mace, half an ounce of nutmegs, a quarter of an ounce of cloves, and half an ounce of black-pepper, all beat fine together, two large spoonfuls of salt, and then mix them together.

Open the fowls all down the back, and bone them; first the pigeon, then the partridge; cover them; then the fowls then the goose, and then the turkey, which must be large; season them all well first, and lay them in the crust, so as it, will look only like a whole turkey.

Then have a hare ready cased, and wiped with a clean cloth. Cut it to pieces, that is, joint it; season it, and lay it as close as you can on one side; on the other side woodcocks, moor game, and what sort of wildfowl you can get. Season them well, and lay them close.

Put at least four pounds of butter into the pie, then lay on your lid, which must be a very thick one, and let it be well baked. It must have a very hot oven, and will take at least four hours. This crust will take a bushel of flour. In this chapter you will see how to make it. These pies are often sent to London in a box, as presents; therefore, the walls must be well built.

~Hannah Glasse

Egg and Bacon Pye to eat cold.

Steep a few thin slices of bacon all night in water to take out the salt, lay your bacon in the dish, beat eight eggs, with a pint of thick cream, put in a little pepper and salt, and pour it on the bacon, lay over it a good cold paste, baked a day before you want it in a moderate oven.

~Elizabeth Raffald

Vegetables

To boil a Collyflower.

Wash and clean your collyflower, boil it in plenty of milk and water (but no salt) till it be tender; when you dish it up, lay greens under it; pour over it good melted butter, and fend it up hot.

~Elizabeth Raffald

To boil Brocoli in Imitation of Asparagus.

TAKE the side shoots of brocoli, strip off the leaves, and with a pen-knife take off all the outrind up to the heads, tie them in bunches, and put them in salt and water, have ready a pan of boiling water, with a handful of salt in it, boil them ten minutes; then lay them in bunches, and pour over them good melted butter.

~Elizabeth Raffald

To Stew Cucumbers.

Take fix large cucumbers, slice them; take six large onions, peel and cut them in thin slices, fry them both brown. Then drain them and pour out the fat. Put them into the pan again, with three spoonfuls of hot water, a quarter of a pound of butter rolled in flour, and a tea spoonful of mustard. Season with pepper and salt, and let them stew a quarter of an hour softly, shaking the pan often. When they are enough dish them up.

~Hannah Glasse

Fried Celery.

Take fix or eight heads of celery; cut off the green tops, and take off the outside stalks, wash them clean, and pare the roots clean; then have ready half a pint of white wine, the yolks of three eggs beat fine, and a little salt and nutmeg; mix all well together with flour into a batter, dip every head into the batter and fry them in butter. When enough, lay them in your dish, and pour melted butter over them.

~*Hannah Glasse*

Bubble and Squeak.

Is made from the remains of boiled salt beef left from a former dinner. Cut the beef in neat slices, and put it between two plates till wanted; if there is any cabbage left from the last dinner it will answer the purpose; it should be squeezed very dry, and then chopped very fine.

Put a little clean dripping into the frying pan; when hot, put in the beef; sprinkle with a very little pepper, and fry it off a nice brown; season both sides. When the beef is done, take it up and put it to keep hot while the cabbage is frying. The cabbage should be kept stirring about while over the fire; it should be fried until all the fat is dried up; put the cabbage on the middle of the dish. Put the beef around it.

~*Eliza Rundell*

Colcannon.

Boil potatoes and greens, or spinage, separately. Mash the potatoes, squeeze the greens dry, chop them quite fine, and mix them with the potatoes with a little butter, pepper, and salt.

Put it into a mould, greasing it well first; let it stand in a hot oven for ten minutes.

~*Eliza Rundell*

✻ PLUM PUDDING AND MINCE PIE

Firmity.

Take a quart of ready-boiled wheat, two quarts of milk, a quarter of a pound of currants clean picked and washed: stir these together and boil them; beat up the yolks of three or four eggs, a little nutmeg, with two or three spoonfuls of milk, and add to the wheat; stir them together for a few minutes. Then sweeten to your palate, and send it to table. ~*Hannah Glasse*

Plum Pottage for Christmas.

Put a leg and shin of beef into eight gallons of water, and boil them till they are very tender. When the broth is strong, strain it out; then wipe the pots, and put in the broth again.

Slice six penny loaves thin, cut off the tops and bottoms, put some of the liquor to them, and cover them up, and let them stand for a quarter of an hour. Then boil and strain it, and put it into your pot. Let them boil a little, and then put in five pounds of stewed raisins of the sun, and two pounds of prunes; let it boil a quarter of an hour.

Then then put in five pounds of currants clean washed and picked. Let these boil till they swell, and then put in three quarters of an ounce of mace, half an ounce of cloves, and two nutmegs, all beat fine. Before you put these into the pot, mix them with a little cold liquor, and do not put them in but a little while before you take off the pot. When you take off the pot, put in three pounds of sugar, a little salt, a quart of sack, a quart of claret, and the juice of two or three lemons. You may thicken with sage instead of bread, if you please. Pour your pottage into earthen pans, and keep it for use.

~John Perkins

A boiled Plum Pudding (18th century)

Take a pound of suet cut in little pieces, not too fine, a pound of currants and a pound of raisins storied, eight eggs, half the whites, half a nutmeg grated and a tea spoonful of beaten ginger, a pound of flour, a pint of milk.

Beat the eggs first, then half the milk. Beat them together and by degrees stir in the flour then the suet, spice and fruit and as much milk as will mix it well together very thick. Boil it five hours.

~*Hannah Glasse*

Rich Plum Pudding (19th Century)

Stone carefully one pound of the best raisins, wash and pick one pound of currants, chop very small one pound of fresh beef suet, blanch and chop small or pound two ounces of sweet almonds and one ounce of bitter ones; mix the whole well together, with one pound of sifted flour, and the same weight of crumb of bread soaked in milk, then squeezed dry and stirred with a spoon until reduced to a mash before it is mixed with the flour.

Cut in small pieces two ounces each of preserved citron, orange, and lemon-peel, and add a quarter of an ounce of mixed spice; quarter of a pound of moist sugar should be put into a basin, with eight eggs, and well beaten together with a three-pronged fork; stir this with the pudding, and make it of a proper consistence with milk.

Remember that it must not be made too thin, or the fruit will sink to the bottom, but be made to the consistence of good thick batter.

Two wineglassfuls of brandy should be poured over the fruit and spice, mixed together in a basin and allowed to stand three or four hours before the pudding is made, stirring them occasionally.

It must be tied in a cloth, and will take five hours of constant boiling. When done, turn it out on a dish, sift loaf-sugar over the top, and serve it with wine-sauce in a boat, and some poured round the pudding. The pudding will be of considerable size, but half the quantity of materials, used in the same proportion, will be equally good.

~*Sarah Hale*

To make Mince-Pies the best way

Take three pounds of suet shred very fine, and chopped as small as possible; two pounds of raisins stoned, and chopped as fine as possible; two pounds of currants nicely picked, washed, rubbed, and dried at the fire; half a hundred of fine pippins, pared, cored, and chopped small; half a pound of fine sugar pounded fine; a quarter of an ounce of mace, a quarter of an ounce of cloves, two large nutmegs, all beat fine; put all together into a great pan, and mix it well together with half a pint of brandy, and half a pint of sack; put it down close in a stone pot, and it will keep good four months.

When you make your pies, take a little dish, something bigger than a soup plate, lay a very thin crust all over it, lay a thin layer of meat, and then a thin layer of citron cut very thin, then a layer of mince-meat, and a layer of orange-peel cut thin, over that a little meat, squeeze half the juice of a fine Seville orange or lemon, lay on your crust, and bake it nicely.

These pies eat finely cold. If you make them in little patties, mix your meat and sweet-meats accordingly. If you choose meat in your pies, parboil a neat's tongue, peel it, and chop the meat as fine as possible, and mix with the rest; or two pounds of the inside of a sirloin of beef boiled. But you must double the quantity of fruit when you use meat.

~*Hannah Glasse*

A Mince Pye.

Boil a neat's tongue two hours, then skin it, and chop it as small as possible, chop very small three pounds of fresh beef suet, three pounds of good baking apples, four pounds of currants clean washed, picked, and well dried before the fire, one pound of jar raisins stoned, and chopped small, and one pound of powder sugar, mix them all together with half an ounce of mace, the same of nutmeg grated, cloves and cinnamon a quarter of an ounce of each, and one pint of French Brandy, and make a rich puff paste; as you fill the pye up, put in a little candied citron and orange cut in little pieces, what you have to spare; put close down in a pot and cover it up, put no citron or orange in till you use it.

~*Elizabeth Raffald*

To make a Mince Pye without Meat.

Chop fine three pounds of suet, and three pounds of apples, when pared and cored, wash and dry three pounds of currants, stone and chop one pound of jar raisins, beat and sift one pound and a half of loaf sugar, cut small twelve ounces of candied orange peel, and fix ounces of citron, mix all well together with a quarter of an ounce of nutmeg, half a quarter of an ounce of cinnamon, fix or eight cloves, and half a pint of French brandy, pot it close up, and keep it for use.

~*Elizabeth Raffald*

❋ SWEET DISHES

Black Butter
This is a very nice preserve to spread on bread for children and much healthier in the winter than salt butter. Take any kind of berries, currants, or cherries (the latter must be stoned)—to every pound of fruit allow half a pound of sugar, and boil till it is reduced on fourth.

Biscuits

To make common Biscuits.
Beat eight eggs half an hour, put in a pound of sugar, beat and sifted, with the rind of a lemon grated, whisk it an hour till it looks light, then put in a pound of flour, with a little rose water, and bake them in tins, or on papers, with sugar over them.

~Elizabeth Raffald

To make Macaroons.
To one pound of blanched and beaten sweet almonds, put one pound of sugar, and a little rose water, to keep them from oiling, then beat the whites of seven eggs to a froth, put them in and beat them well together, drop them on wafer paper, grate sugar over them, and bake them.

~Elizabeth Raffald

To make Shrewsbury Cakes.
Take two pounds of flour, a pound of sugar finely searced (sifted), mix them together (take out a quarter

of a pound to roll them in); take four eggs beat, four spoonfuls of cream, and two spoonfuls of rose-water; beat them well together, and mix them with the flour into a paste, roll them into thin cakes, and bake them in a quick oven.

~*Hannah Glasse*

Naples Biscuit.

Put three quarters of a pound of very fine flour to a pound of fine beaten sugar; sift it three times, then add six eggs well beat, and a spoonful of rose-water: when the oven is almost hot, make them; but take care that they are not made up too wet.

~*John Perkins*

Sugar Cakes.

Take a pound and a half of very fine flour, one pound of cold butter, half a pound of sugar, work all these well together into a paste, then roll it with the palms of your hands into balls, and cut them with a glass into cakes; lay them in a sheet of paper, with some flour under them: to bake them you may make tumblets, only blanch in almonds, and beat them small, and lay them in the midst of a long piece of paste, and roll it round with your fingers, and cast them into knots, in what fashion you please; prick them and bake them.

~*Hannah Glasse*

Cakes

Twelfth Night Cakes

Formal recipes for Twelfth Cake do not appear in print until 1803. The Rich Cake and Icing recipes might have been used prior to that. In either case, the recipes make very large, cakes. The first recipe produces something more akin to modern fruit cakes. The later results in something lighter, more like the modern sweet bread. Neither yields a soft, fluffy pastry resembling a modern cake.

To Make a Rich Cake.

Take four pounds of flour dried and sifted, seven pounds of currants washed and rubbed, six pounds of the best fresh butter, two pounds of Jordan almonds blanched, and beaten with orange flower water and sack till fine; then take four pounds of eggs, put half the whites away, three pounds of double-refined sugar beaten and sifted, a quarter of an ounce of mace, the same of cloves and cinnamon, three large nutmegs, all beaten fine, a little ginger, half a pint of sack, half a pint of right French brandy, sweet-meats to your liking, they must be orange, lemon, and citron.

Work your butter to a cream with your hands before any of your ingredients are in; then put in your sugar, and mix all well together; let your eggs be well beat and strained through a sieve, work in your almonds first, then put in your eggs, beat them together till they look white and thick; then put in your sack, brandy and spices, shake your flour in be degrees, and when your oven is ready, put in your currants and sweet-meats as you put it in your hoop.

It will take four hours baking in a quick oven: you must keep it beating with your hand all the while you are mixing of it, and when your currants are well washed and cleaned, let them be kept before the fire, so that they may go warm into your cake. This quantity will bake best in two hoops.

~*Hannah Glasse*

Almond icing.

Take the whites of six eggs, a pound and half of double refined sugar; beat a pound of Jordan almonds, blanch them, and pound fine in a little rose water; mix all together, and whisk it well for an hour or two; then lay over your cake, and put it in an oven.

~ *John Perkins*

To make red colouring for Pippin Paste, &c. For garnishing Twelfth Cakes.

Take an ounce of cochineal beat very fine; add three gills of water, a quarter of an ounce of rock-alum, and two ounces of lump sugar; boil them together for twenty minutes, strain it through a fine sieve, and preserve it for use close covered.

~*John Simpson*

Twelfth Cakes.

Take seven pounds of flour, make a cavity in the center, set a sponge with a gill and a half of yeast and a little warm milk; then put round it one pound of fresh butter broke into small lumps, one pound and a quarter of sifted sugar, four pounds and a half of currants washed and picked, half an ounce of sifted cinnamon, a quarter of an ounce of pounded cloves, mace, and nutmeg mixed, sliced candied orange or lemon peel and citron.

When the sponge is risen mix all the ingredients together with a little warm milk; let the hoops be well papered and buttered, then fill them with the mixture and bake them, and when nearly pound and a quarter of sifted sugar, tour pounds and a half of currants washed and picked, half an ounce of sifted cinnamon, a quarter of an ounce of pounded cloves, mace, and nutmeg mixed, sliced candied orange or lemon peel and citron.

When the sponge is risen mix all the ingredients together with a little warm milk; let the hoops be well papered and buttered, then fill them with the mixture and bake them, and when nearly cold, ice them over with sugar prepared for that purpose as per receipt; or they may be plain.

~*John Simpson*

~ Robert Chambers, *Book of Day*

To make little fine Cakes.

One pound of butter beaten to cream, a pound and a quarter of flour, a pound of fine sugar beat fine, a pound of currants clean washed and picked, six eggs, two whites left out; beat them fine, mix the flour, sugar, and eggs by degrees into the batter, beat it all well with both hands; either make into little cakes, or bake it in one.

~*Hannah Glasse*

Heart cakes.

Work a pound of butter with the hand to a cream; put to it a dozen yolks of egg, and half the whites, well beaten, a pound of flour dried, a pound of sifted sugar, four spoonfuls of good brandy, and a pound of currants washed, and dried before the fire.

As the pans are filled, put in two ounces of candied orange and citron; continue beating the cakes till they go into the oven. This quantity will fill three dozen of middling pans.

~*John Perkins*

To make Ginger-Bread Cakes.

Take three pounds of flour, one pound of sugar, one pound of butter rubbed in very fine, two ounces of ginger beat fine, a large nutmeg grated. Then take a pound of treacle, a quarter of a pint of cream, make them warm together, and make up the bread stiff.

Roll it out, and make it up into thin wakes, cut them out with a tea-cup, or small glass; or roll them round like nuts, and bake them on tin-plates in a quick oven.

~*Hannah Glasse*

Molded Jellies

Molded jellies were a favorite fancy dessert. They could be made in plain, utilitarian shapes, but they reached their heights when prepared in beautiful molded forms, sometimes layered with multiple flavors or colors, or even housing fruits or flowers inside.

Without the modern advantaged of prepackaged gelatins, Regency Era cooks had to obtain their gelatin from deer antlers, isinglass (from the dried swim bladders of fish) and calves feet.

Orange-Jelly.

Take half a pound of hartshorn shavings, or four ounces of isinglass, and boil it in spring-water till it is of a strong jelly; take the juice of three Seville oranges, three lemons, and six china oranges, and the rind of one Seville orange, and one lemon pared very thin; put them to your jelly.

Sweeten it with loaf-sugar to your palate; beat up the whites of eight eggs to a froth, and mix well in, then boil it for ten minutes, then run it through a jelly-bag till it is very clear, and put it in moulds till cold, then dip your mould in warm water, and turn it out into a china dish, or a flat glass, and garnish with flowers.

~*Hannah Glasse*

To make Ribband-Jelly.

Take out the great bones of four calves feet, put the feet into a pot with ten quarts of water, three ounces of hartshorn, three ounces of isinglass, a nutmeg quartered, and four blades of mace; then boil this till it comes to two quarts, strain it through a flannel bag, let it stand twenty-four hours.

Then scrape off all the fat from the top very clean, then slice it, put to it the whites of fix eggs beaten to a froth, boil it a little, and strain it through a flannel bag.

Then run the jelly into little high glasses, run every colour as thick as your finger, one colour must be thorough cold before you put another on, and that you put on must be but blood-warm, for fear it mix together. You must colour red with cochineal, green with spinach, yellow with saffron, blue with syrup of violets, white with thick cream, and sometimes the jelly by itself. You may add orange-flower water, or wine and sugar, and lemon, if you, please; but this is all fancy.

~*Hannah Glasse*

To make Calves-Feet Jelly.

Boil two calves feet in a gallon of water till it comes to a quart, then strain it, let it stand till cold, skim off all the fat clean, and take the jelly up clean. If there is any settling in the bottom, leave it.

Put the jelly into a sauce-pan, with a pint of mountain-wine, half a pound of loaf-sugar, the juice of four large lemons; beat up fix or eight whites of eggs with a whisk, then put them into a sauce-pan, and stir all together well till it boils.

Let it boil a few minutes. Have ready a large flannel bag, pour it in, it will run through quick, pour it in again till it runs clear, then have ready a large china basin, with the lemon-peels cut as thin as possible, let the jelly run into that basin; and the peels both give it a fine amber colour, and also a flavour; with a clean silver spoon fill your glasses.

~*Hannah Glasse*

Blanc mange.

Pick three ounces of isinglass, put it in a stew-pan, with a pint of boiling water; let it simmer on a slow fire till it is quite dissolved; add to it a quart of cream, a stick of cinnamon, a few coriander seeds, the rind of a lemon pared very thin, and two laurel leaves. Boil for three minutes, and sweeten to your taste. Take it off, strain through a sieve, and keep stirring it till almost cold; then do your moulds with a little sweet oil, wipe them with a clean cloth, and put in the blanc mange; let it stand till cold and stiff, loosen it round the edges of the mould with a pin, lay it carefully in a dish, and serve it up.

If you choose to have your blanc mange of a green colour, put in as much juice of spinach as will be necessary for that purpose, and a spoonful of brandy; but it should not then retain the name of blanc mange (white food), but verde mange (green food). If you would have it yellow, dissolve a little saffron in it; you should then call it jaune mange. Or you may make it red, by putting a piece of cochineal into a little brandy, let it stand half an hour, and strain it through a bit of cloth: it is then entitled to the appellation of rouge mange.

~*John Perkins*

To make Apple-Dumplings.

Make a good puff-paste, pare some large apples, cut them in quarters; and take out the cores very nicely; take a piece of crust, and roll it round, enough for one apple; if they are big, they will not look pretty; so roll the crust found each apple, and make them sound like a ball, with a little flour in your hand.

Have a pot of water boiling, take a clean cloth; dip it in the water; and shake flour over it; tie each dumpling by itself, and put them in the water boiling; which keep boiling all the time; and if your crust is light and good, and the apples not too large, half an hour will boil them; but if the apples be large, they will take an hour's boiling.

When they are enough, take them up, and lay them in a dish; throw fine sugar all over them, and send them to table. Have good fresh butter melted in a cup, and fine beaten sugar in a saucer.

~Elizabeth Raffald

To make a Trifle.

Put three large maccaroons in the middle of your dish, pour as much white wine over them as they will drink, then take a quart of cream, put in as much sugar as will make it sweet, rub your sugar upon the rind of a lemon to fetch out the essence.

Put your cream into a pot, mill it to a strong froth, lay as much froth upon a sieve as will fill the dish you intend to put your trifle in, put the remainder of your cream into a tossing pan, with a stick of cinnamon, the yolks of four eggs well beat, and sugar to your taste, set them over a gentle fire, stir it one way till it is thick, then take it off the fire, pour it upon your macaroons.

When it is cold put on your frothed cream, lay round it different coloured sweetmeats, and small shot comfits in, and figures or flowers.

~ *Elizabeth Raffald*

To make a Trifle.

Cover the bottom of your dish or bowl with Naples biscuits broke in pieces, macaroons broke in halves, and ratafia cakes. Just wet them all through with sack.

Then make a good boiled custard, not too thick, and when cold, pour it over it, then put a syllabub over that. You may garnish it with ratafia cakes, currant jelly, and flowers, and strew different coloured nonpareils over it. Note, these are bought at the confectioners. ~*Hannah Glasse*

Almond Paste, for Second Course Dishes.

Take a pound of sweet and four ounces of biter almonds. Blanch them and make them as dry as you can, put them into a mortar and pound them well, beat up the whites of three eggs, and wet the almonds with it by a little at a time.

When pounded enough, rub it through a tammy sieve, then get a small preserving pan, set it over a stove, not very fierce and put the almonds in the pan.

Stir in a pound of very fine sifted treble refined sugar, or as much as w1ll bring it to a paste consistence; take it out of the preserving and put it between two plates to sweat.

When cold, make it into what shapes you think proper; there are shells of different sorts for almond paste. ... Make some into cups, like coffee cups and cream jugs, or anything your fancy will lead you, for that must be the guide for all these kind of things.

~*John Simpson*

To make Ice-Cream.

Pare and stone twelve ripe apricots, and scald them, beat them fine in a mortar, add to them fix ounces of double-refined sugar, and a pint of scalding cream, and work it through a sieve; put it in a tin with a close cover, and set it in a tub of ice broken small, with four handfuls of salt mixed among the ice. When you see your cream grows thick round the edges of your tin, stir it well, and put it in again till it is quite thick; when the cream is all froze up, take it out of the tin, and put it into the mould you intend to turn it out of; put on the lid, and have another tub of salt and ice ready as before; put the mould in the middle, and lay the ice under and over it; let it stand four hours, and never turn it out till the moment you want it, then dip the mould in cold spring-water, and turn it into a plate. You may do any sort of fruit the same way.

~Hannah Glasse

❈ BEVERAGES

Syllabub

Syllabub had several forms, but in all, it was a mixture of alcohol and cream, less potent than egg nog. Some recipes call for making it directly under the cow, but Hannah Glasse recommends other less rustic alternatives.

To make Whipped-Syllabubs.

Take a quart of thick cream, and half a pint of sack, the juice of two Seville oranges or lemons, grate in the peel of two lemons, half a pound of double-refined sugar, pour it into a broad earthen pan, and whisk it well; but first sweeten some red-wine or sack, and fill your glasses as full as you choose, then as the froth rises, take it off with a spoon, and lay it on a sieve to drain; then lay it carefully into your glasses till they are as full as they will hold.

Do not make these long before you use them. Many use cider sweetened, or any wine you please, or lemon, or orange whey made thus: squeeze the juice of a lemon, or orange, into a quarter of a pint of milk; when the curd is hard, pour the whey clear off, and sweeten it to your palate. You may colour some with the juice of spinach, some with saffron, and some with cochineal, just as you fancy

~*Hannah Glasse*

To make Solid Syllabub.

To a quart of rich cream put a pint of white-wine, the juice of two lemons, the rind of one grated, sweeten it to your taste; mill it with a chocolate mill till it is all of a thickness; then put it in glasses, or a bowl, and set it in a cool place till next day.

~*Hannah Glasse*

Syllabub under the Cow.

Put into a punch bowl a pint of cider, and a bottle of strong beer; grate in a small nutmeg, and sweeten it to your taste; then milk from the cow as much milk as will make a strong froth. Then let it stand an hour; strew over it a few currants well washed, picked, and plumped before the fire, and it will be fit for service.

~*John Perkins*

Punch

Punch was the most popular drink to share with company during Jane Austen's day. The name punch derived from a Persian and Hindu words, a reflection of the trade with the Far East that brought the necessary spices to Europe.

Hostesses found the beverage expensive and difficult to prepare. Citrus fruit had to be carefully pared, juiced, and the juice sieved. The sugar, spices and spirits added to the juices were costly ingredients, often kept under lock and key by the mistress of the house.

Norfolk Punch

In twenty quarts of French brandy put the peel of thirty lemons and thirty oranges, pared so thin that not the least of the white is left. Infuse twelve hours. Have ready thirty quarts of cold water that has boiled;

put to it fifteen pounds of double refined sugar; and when well mixed, pour it upon the brandy and peels, adding the juice of the oranges and of twenty-four lemons; mix well. Then strain through a very fine hair-sieve, into a very clean barrel that has held spirits, and put two quarts of new milk.

Stir and then bung it close; let it stand six weeks in a warm cellar; bottle the liquor for use, observing great care that the bottles are perfectly clean and dry, and the corks of the best quality, and well put in. This liquor will keep many years, and improves by age.

~*Eliza Rundell*

Bottled punch.

Take a gallon of good brandy, and put to it the parings of six lemons, and as many oranges; let them infuse for four days.

In the meantime, take six quarts of soft water, and a pound and a half of fine sugar, with the whites of six eggs, beaten up to a froth in a little of the cold water mix them together, and set the liquor over the fire, and when it boils scum it, as long as any scum rises.

Then set it by till it is cold, and then put it up into a proper vessel, and add to it the brandy with the peels, and as much of the pieces of lemon as you think fit; stop up the vessel close and let it stand for six weeks; then rack it for use.

This is a strong punch to be used only as a cordial dram of a grateful taste and flavour, and is sold in some taverns under a foreign name.

~*John Perkins*

~William Hogarth,. *A Midnight Modern Conversation.*

Verder or Milk Punch

Pare six oranges, and six lemons, as thin as you can, grate them after with sugar to get the flavour. Steep the peels in a bottle of rum or brandy stopped close twenty four hours. Squeeze the fruit on two pounds of sugar, add to it four quarts of water, and one of new milk boiling hot; stir the rum into the above, and run it through a jelly-bag till perfectly clear. Bottle and cork close immediately.

~Eliza Rundell

Ratafia.

Blanch two ounces of peach and apricot kernels, bruise and put them into a bottle, and fill nearly up with brandy. Dissolve half a pound of white sugar-candy in a cup of cold water, and add to the brandy after it has stood a month on the kernels, and they are strained off. Then filter through paper, and bottle for use.

~Eliza Rundell

To make negus.

Ingredients – To every pint of port wine allow 1 quart of boiling water, 1/4 lb. of sugar, 1 lemon, grated nutmeg to taste.

Mode.—As this beverage is more usually drunk at children's parties than at any other, the wine need not be very old or expensive for the purpose, a new fruity wine answering very well for it. Put the wine into a jug, rub some lumps of sugar (equal to 1/4 lb.) on the lemon-rind until all the yellow part of the skin is absorbed, then squeeze the juice, and strain it. Add the sugar and lemon-juice to the port wine, with the grated nutmeg; pour over it the boiling water, cover the jug, and, when the beverage has cooled a little, it will be fit for use. Negus may also be made of sherry, or any other sweet white wine, but is more usually made of port than of any other beverage.

~Mrs. Beeton

References

Ackermann, Rudolph. *Collection of Fashion Plates from Ackermann's Repository of Arts, Literature, Commerce, Manufactures, Fashions, and Politics.* 1814.

Ayto, John, and John Ayto. *An A-Z of Food and Drink.* Oxford: Oxford University Press, 2002.

Beeton, Isabella. *Beeton's Book of Household Management.* London: S. O. Beeton Publishing, 1861.

Bell, John. *Fashion Plate (French Dinner Party Dress).* 1821. Print, paper. Los Angeles County Museum of Art, Los Angeles.

Beverley, Jo. "Christmas in the Regency." Welcome to Jo Beverley's World. Accessed October 28, 2014. http://jobev.com/xmasarticle.html.

Black, Maggie, and Deirdre Faye. *The Jane Austen Cookbook.* Chicago, Ill: Chicago Review Press, 1995.

Boyle, Laura. "The Origins of Regency Era Christmas Carols." Jane Austen. June 20, 2011. Accessed October 28, 2014. http://www.janeausten.co.uk/the-origins-of-regency-era-christmas-carols/.

Boyle, Laurra. "The Regency Card Party." Jane Austen .co.uk. June 20, 2011. Accessed November 5, 2014. http://www.janeausten.co.uk/the-regency-card-party/ .

Broomfield, Andrea. *Food and Cooking in Victorian England: A History*. Westport, Conn.: Praeger Publishers, 2007.

Bourne, Joanna. "Caroling, Caroling in the Regency." Word Wenches. December 29, 2012. Accessed October 28, 2014.
http://wordwenches.typepad.com/word_wenches/2012/12/caroling-caroling.html.

Byrne, Paula. *Jane Austen in Context*. Cambridge: Cambridge University Press, 2005.

Chambers, Robert. *The Book of Days; a Miscellany of Popular Antiquities in Connection with the Calendar, including Anecdote, Biography & History, Curiosities of Literature, and Oddities of Human Life and Character,*. Detroit: Gale Research, 1967.

Davidson, Alan. *The Oxford Companion to Food*. Oxford: Oxford University Press, 1999.

Day, Malcom. *Voices from the World of Jane Austen*. David and Charles, 2006.

Downing, Sarah Jane. *Fashion in the Time of Jane Austen*. Oxford: Shire Publications, 2010.

Faye, Deirdre. *Jane Austen: The World of Her Novels*. New York: Abrams, 2002.

"First Footing and Hogmanay, a Truly Scottish New Year!" HubPages. January 1, 2011. Accessed October 28, 2014.
http://diffugerenives.hubpages.com/hub/First-footing-and-Hogmanay-a-truly-Scottish-New-Year.

Gilbert, Davies. *Some Ancient Christmas Carols, with the Tunes to Which They Were Formerly Sung in the West of*

England. Together with Two Ancient Ballads, a Dialogue, &c. 2d ed. London: Printed by J. Nichols and Son, 1823.

Glasse, Hannah. *The Art of Cookery, Made Plain and Easy: Which Far Exceeds Any Thing of the Kind Ever Yet Published* ... London: Printed for the Author, and Sold at Mrs. Ashburn's, a China Shop, the Corner of Fleet-Ditch, 1747.

Glasse, Hannah. *The Art of Cookery Made Plain and Easy: Which Far Exceeds Any Thing of the Kind Yet Published* ... *To Which Are Added, One Hundred and Fifty New and Useful Receipts. And Also Fifty Receipts for Different Articles of Perfumery. With a Copious Index* ... New ed. London: Printed for W. Strahan, J. Rivington and Sons, L. Davis [and 23 Others], 1784.

Griffen, Robert H., and Ann H. Shurgin, eds. *The Folklore of World Holidays.* Second ed. Detroit: Gale, 1998. P. 679.

Hale, Sarah Josepha Buell. *Lady's Book.* Philadelphia:: Published by L.A. Godey, 1860.

Hazzard, Kieran. "A Regency Christmas." 95th Rifles. January 1, 2013. Accessed October 28, 2014. http://www.95th-rifles.co.uk/research/a-regency-christmas/.

Hirst, Christopher. "Sweet Delight: A Brief History of the Mince Pie." The Independent. December 4, 2011. Accessed October 28, 2014. http://www.independent.co.uk/life-style/food-and-drink/features/sweet-delight-a-brief-history-of-the-mince-pie-6270572.html.

Hogarth, William. *A Midnight Modern Conversation*. 1730. Print, paper. Private Collection, n.p.

"Hogmanay / Old Years Night / New Years Day." Walkabout Crafts' Accessed October 28, 2014. http://www.walkaboutcrafts.com/worldtour/scotlan d/festivals/hogmanay.htm.

Hubert Von Staufer, Maria. "Black Butter." The Christmas Archives. March 1, 1995. Accessed October 28,2014.
http://www.christmasarchives.com/black_butter.html.

Jones, Hazel. *Jane Austen and Marriage*. London: Continuum, 2009.

Kane, Kathryn. "Dancing the Easter Carols." The Regency Redingote. December 23, 2011. Accessed October 28, 2014.
http://regencyredingote.wordpress.com/2011/12/23 /dancing-the-easter-carols/.

Kane, Kathryn. "The Fine Art of Toasting in the Regency." The Regency Redingote. March 15, 2013. Accessed November 5, 2014.
http://regencyredingote.wordpress.com/2013/03/15 /the-fine-art-of-toasting-in-the-regency/.

Kane, Kathryn. "The Yule Candle in the Regency." The Regency Redingote. January 24, 2010. Accessed October 28, 2014.
http://regencyredingote.wordpress.com/2010/12/24 /the-yule-candle-in-the-regency/.

Knightly, Charles. *The Customs and Ceremonies of Britain*. London: Thames and Hudson, 1986.

Knowles, Rachel. "An Unusual Gift Idea for Your Parents for Christmas 1813." Regency History. December 7, 2012. Accessed October 28, 2014. http://www.regencyhistory.net/2012/12/an-unusual-gift-idea-for-your-parents.html.

Knowles, Rachel. "Did They Have Christmas Trees in the Regency?" Regency History. December 15, 2012. Accessed October 28, 2014. http://www.regencyhistory.net/2012/12/did-they-have-christmas-trees-in-regency.html.

Koster, Kristen. "A Regency Primer on Christmastide & New Year's." Kristen Koster. December 27, 2011. Accessed October 28, 2014. http://www.kristenkoster.com/2011/12/a-regency-primer-on-christmastide-new-years/.

Koster, Kristen. "A Regency Primer on Twelfth Night & Wassailing." Kristen Koster. January 3, 2012. Accessed October 28, 2014. http://www.kristenkoster.com/2012/01/a-regency-primer-on-twelfth-night-wassailing/.

Lane, Maggie. *Jane Austen and Food*. London: Hambledon Press, 1995.

Lane, Maggie. *Jane Austen's World: The Life and times of England's Most Popular Novelist*. 2nd ed. London: Carlton Books, 2005.

Lane, Sarah. "History and Tradition of Christmas Pudding." Class Brain. November 17, 2008. Accessed October 28, 2014. http://www.classbrain.com/artholiday/publish/printer_article_256.shtml.

Larson, Tomm. "The Yule Log." Noel Noel Noel. Accessed October 28, 2014. http://www.noelnoelnoel.com/trad/yulelog.html.

Laudermilk, Sharon H., and Teresa L. Hamlin. *The Regency Companion*. New York: Garland, 1989.

Marks, J. L. *Theatrical Portrait - Mr Ellar as Harlequin.* (1822 - 1839). Print, paper. Museum of London, London, UK, Europe.

Mayer, Nancy. "Christmas Day." Nancy Regency Researcher. Accessed October 28, 2014.

http://www.regencyresearcher.com/pages/christmas 1.html.

Mayer, Nancy. "Christmas Pantomimes." Nancy Regency Researcher. Accessed October 28, 2014. http://www.regencyresearcher.com/pages/christmas pant.html.

Mayer, Nancy. "Emma's Christmas Lists." Nancy Regency Researcher. Accessed October 28, 2014. http://www.regencyresearcher.com/pages/christmasl ist.html.

"Mince Pie History." Mince Pie Club. Accessed November 10, 2013.
http://www.mincepieclub.co.uk/Mince_Pie_News/ Mince_Pie_History/The_History_Of_The_Mince_Pi e.html.

Mollard, John. *The Art of Cookery Made Easy and Refined: Comprising Ample Directions for Preparing Every Article Requisite for Furnishing the Tables of the Nobleman, Gentleman, and Tradesman.* 3rd ed. London: Printed for the Author, and Sold by J. Nunn, 1807.

Norwich. *The Gentleman and Lady's Companion; Containing the Newest Cotilions and Country Dances; to Which Is Added Instance of Ill Manners to Be Carefully Avoided by Youth of Both Sexes*. London: J. Trumbull, 1798.

Oliver, Lynne. "The Food Timeline--Christmas Food History." The Food Timeline. January 1, 2002. Accessed October 28, 2014.
http://www.foodtimeline.org/christmasfood.html.

Parkes, Mrs. William. *Domestic Duties; Or, Instructions To Young Married Ladies.* London: Longman, Hurst. Rees, Orme, Brown, And Green, 1824.

Parley, Peter. *Tales about Christmas.* London: Chiswick Press, 1838.

Perkins, John. *Every Woman Her Own House-keeper; Or, The Ladies' Library Containing the Cheapest and Most Extensive System of Cookery Ever Offered to the Public. ... Also, The Family Physician; Or, A Complete Body of Domestic Medicine.* 4th ed. London: James Ridgway, 1796.

Raffald, Elizabeth. *The Experienced English Housekeeper for the Use and Ease of Ladies, Housekeepers, Cooks, &c. Written Purely from Practice ... Consisting of near Nine Hundred Original Receipts, Most of Which Never Appeared in Print. ... The Tenth Edition. ... By Elizabeth Raffald.* London: Printed for R. Baldwin, 1786.

Ray, Joan Klingel. *Jane Austen for Dummies.* Chichester: John Wiley, 2006.

"Regency Christmas Traditions: Hogmanay." November 26, 2013. Accessed December 10, 2013. http://trsparties.com/2013/11/26/regency-christmas-traditions-hogmanay/.

Regency Etiquette: The Mirror of Graces (1811). Enl. ed. Mendocino, CA: R.L. Shep;, 1997.

Rendell, Jane. *The Pursuit of Pleasure Gender, Space & Architecture in Regency London.* London: Athlone Press;, 2002.

Revel, Rachel. *Winter Evening Pastimes; Or, the Merry-maker's Companion Containing a Complete Collection of Evening Sports, including Twelfth-night Ceremonies, with Copious Directions for Crying Forfeits, and Promoting Harmless Mirth and Innocent Amusement. The Whole Selected, Altered, and Composed, by Rachel Revel, Spinster.* London: Printed for A. Mesnard, 40, Strand, 1825.

Ross, Josephine, and Henrietta Webb. *Jane Austen's Guide to Good Manners: Compliments, Charades & Horrible Blunders.* New York: Bloomsbury USA, 2006.

Rowlandson, Thomas. *Caricature of a Longways Country Dance.* 1790's. Pen and ink. N.p.

Rundell, Maria Eliza Ketelby. *A New System of Domestic Cookery: Formed upon Principles of Economy, and Adapted to the Use of Private Families.* A New ed. London: Printed for John Murray ..., 1814.

Sanborn, Vic. "Black Butter: A Christmas Recipe Popular in Jane Austen's Day." Jane Austen's World. December 12, 2009. Accessed October 28, 2014. https://janeaustensworld.wordpress.com/2009/12/1 2/black-butter-a-christmas-recipe-popular-in-jane-austens-day/.

Sanborn, Vic. "Christmas Pudding." Jane Austen's World. December 19, 2006. Accessed October 28, 2014.http://janeaustensworld.wordpress.com/2006/ 12/19/christmas-pudding/.

Sanborn, Vic. "Syllabub or Sillabub, Straight from the Cow: We Just Don't Drink It Like This Any More." Jane Austen's World. December 19, 2007. Accessed October 28, 2014.

http://janeaustensworld.wordpress.com/2007/12/19 /syllabub-or-sillabub/.

Sanborn, Vic. "Yule Log." Jane Austen's World. December 21, 2006. Accessed October 28, 2014. http://janeaustensworld.wordpress.com/2006/12/21 /yule-log/.

Selwyn, David. *Jane Austen and Leisure*. London: Hambledon Press, 1999.

Simpson, John. *A Complete System of Cookery, on a Plan Entirely New, Consisting of Every Thing That Is Requisite for Cooks to Know in the Kitchen Business; Containing Bills of Fare for Every Day in the Year, and Directions to Dress Each Dish; Being One Year's Work at the Marquis of Buckingham's from the 1st of January to the 31st of December, 1805*. London: Printed for W. Stewart, 1806.

Sinclair, Gary. "Hogmanay." The Mel Sinclair Clan. December 1, 2003. Accessed October 28, 2014. http://www.clansinclairsc.org/hogmanay.htm.

Stradley, Linda. "History of Plum Pudding Plum." What's Cooking America. Accessed October 28, 2014.http://whatscookingamerica.net/Cake/plumpu ddingTips.htm.

Sullivan, Margaret C., and Kathryn Rathke. *The Jane Austen Handbook: Proper Life Skills from Regency England*. Philadelphia, PA: Quirk Books, 2007.

Todd, Janet. *Jane Austen in Context*. Cambridge, UK: Cambridge University Press, 2005.

Trusler, John. *The Honours of the Table or Rules of Behavior during Meals*. 2nd ed. London: Literary Press, 1791.

Vickery, Amanda. *The Gentleman's Daughter: Women's Lives in Georgian England.* New Haven, Conn.: Yale University Press, 1998.

Waugh, Joanna. "Christmas Frivolity." Joanna Waugh. December 13, 2008. Accessed October 28, 2014. http://www.joannawaugh.blogspot.com/2008/12/christmas-frivolity.html.

Waugh, Joanna. "Christmas Feast." Joanna Waugh. December 15, 2008. Accessed October 28, 2014. http://www.joannawaugh.blogspot.com/2008/12/christmas-feast.html.

Waugh, Joanna. "Christmas Gift Giving." Joanna Waugh. December 22, 2008. Accessed October 28, 2014.
http://www.joannawaugh.blogspot.com/2008/12/christmas-gift-giving.html.

Waugh, Joanna. "Decking the Halls." Joanna Waugh. December 11, 2008. Accessed October 28, 2014. http://www.joannawaugh.blogspot.com/2008/12/decking-halls.html.

Wilson, Thomas. *The Complete System of English Country Dancing, Containing All the Figures Ever Used in English Country Dancing, with a Variety of New Figures, and New Reels* ... London: Sherwood, Neeley and Jones, 1815.

"The Yule Log." The Yule Log. Accessed October 28, 2014.http://www.culture.gouv.fr/culture/noel/angl/buche.htm.

Acknowledgments

So many people have helped me along the journey taking this from an idea to a reality.

Abigail, Jan, and Ruth thank you so much for cold reading, proof reading and being honest!

And my dear friend Cathy, my biggest cheerleader, you have kept me from chickening out more than once! Thank you!

Other Books by Maria Grace

Fine Eyes and Pert Opinions
Remember the Past
The Darcy Brothers

A Jane Austen Regency Life Series:
A Jane Austen Christmas: Regency Christmas Traditions
Courtship and Marriage in Jane Austen's World
How Jane Austen Kept her Cook: An A to Z History of
Georgian Ice Cream

Jane Austen's Dragons Series:
A Proper Introduction to Dragons
Pemberley: Mr. Darcy's Dragon
Longbourn: Dragon Entail
Netherfield:Rogue Dragon

The Queen of Rosings Park Series:
Mistaking Her Character
The Trouble to Check Her
A Less Agreeable Man

Sweet Tea Stories:
A Spot of Sweet Tea: Hopes and Beginnings (short story
anthology)
Snowbound at Hartfield
A Most Affectionate Mother
Inspiration

Darcy Family Christmas Series:
Darcy and Elizabeth: Christmas 1811
The Darcy's First Christmas
From Admiration to Love

Given Good Principles Series:
Darcy's Decision
The Future Mrs. Darcy
All the Appearance of Goodness
Twelfth Night at Longbourn

Behind the Scenes Anthologies (with Austen Variations):
Pride and Prejudice: Behind the Scenes
Persuasion: Behind the Scenes

Non-fiction Anthologies
Castles, Customs, and Kings Vol. 1
Castles, Customs, and Kings Vol. 2
Putting the Science in Fiction

Available in e-book, audio book and paperback

On Line Exclusives at:

www.http//RandomBitsofFascination.com

Bonus and deleted scenes
Regency Life Series

Free e-books:

- *Rising Waters: Hurricane Harvey Memoirs*
- *Lady Catherine's Cat*
- *A Gift from Rosings Park*
- *Bits of Bobbin Lace*
- *Half Agony, Half Hope: New Reflections on Persuasion*
- *Four Days in April*

About the Author

Six time BRAG Medallion Honoree, #1 Best-selling Historical Fantasy author Maria Grace has her PhD in Educational Psychology and is a 16-year veteran of the university classroom where she taught courses in human growth and development, learning, test development and counseling. None of which have anything to do with her undergraduate studies in economics/sociology/managerial studies/behavior sciences. She pretends to be a mild-mannered writer/cat-lady, but most of her vacations require helmets and waivers or historical costumes, usually not at the same time.

She writes gaslamp fantasy, historical romance and non-fiction to help justify her research addiction.

Contact Maria Grace:

author.MariaGrace@gmail.com

Facebook:
http://facebook.com/AuthorMariaGrace

On Amazon.com:
http://amazon.com/author/mariagrace

Random Bits of Fascination
(http://RandomBitsofFascination.com)

Austen Variations (http://AustenVariations.com)

English Historical Fiction Authors
(http://EnglshHistoryAuthors.blogspot.com)

White Soup Press (http://whitesouppress.com/)

On Twitter @WriteMariaGrace

On Pinterest: http://pinterest.com/mariagrace423/

❦ Index

121

Made in the USA
Middletown, DE
06 November 2023

42003224R00078